Roxana

FORESTER HOGG

DEDICATION

To Karen, Jody, and Sherri; to Rebecca, Shane, Chelsie, Seth, and Jackson; and in loving memory of Eric.

Table of Contents

ACKNOWLEDGMENTS v
1   INTRODUCTION 1
2   Snakebit from the Start 7
3   Attitudes: Us and Them 11
4   Roxana 23
5   Junk Food and Quack Cures 39
6   Granny Larce's Forty-Some-Odd 45
7   Baby to Angel 53
8   Big Branch 57
9   Pace's Branch 67
10 The Three Rs and a W 85
11 All Aboard 91
12 Cowboys and Haints 103
13 Pie Suppers an' Fightin' 109
14 Earning our Keep 115
15 From Gettin' by to Gettin' Ahead 123
16 Under One Roof Again, Almost 127
17 Keeping One Foot in the Hills 135
18 I Like Ike 143
19 Young Sharecropper 145
20 Before Astroturf or Sports Medicine 147
21 Fledgling Entrepreneur 151
22 The Supporting Cast 155
23 Three Good years 169
24 Fast Forward 185
Afterword 187
ABOUT THE AUTHOR 189

Illustration by Jackson

Jackson's Tree

ACKNOWLEDGMENTS

Artwork

All the illustrations in this book are original drawings by my daughter Jody. She chose scenes from this book to interpret in charcoal drawings and she imbued each of them with her characteristic *joy de vivre*. Thank you, Jody, for seeing beyond the scenes and directly into my heart.

Jackson's Tree

My grandson, Jackson, drew this image for his elementary school art project. I view Jackson's tree as a "family tree", not in a genealogical sense, but as an emblem of a "family" in which most of the links are by blood, and the remaining ones are by rare good fortune.

Graphic Technical Support

For her continuous moral support and invaluable contributions to this book's design and layout, and for pre-press preparation of the artwork, I tender my heartfelt thanks to my friend Rennie.

Photos

My Aunt Gladys (Whitaker) Hogg has long been the historian for both sides of my extended family, the Hoggs and the Whitakers, and I am indebted to her for providing all the older photos used herein.

Proof Reading

I am indebted to my caring and supportive friend Mac for his careful reading that lead to improvements in my book.

AUTHOR'S NOTE

Most of the names in this book are the actual names of the persons I'm writing about. For my blood relatives, with a few minor exceptions, I use their real names. And I give the real names of a few other persons who helped out in times of need. But there are many more who make only brief appearances, and for some of them I have used fictitious names to protect their privacy

1928: My mother and father, Chelsea (Whitaker) Hogg and Hobson Hogg, are newly-weds here. They were married on the front porch of the James Whitaker home at the head of Big Branch. They spent their wedding night there with her family and next day walked across the mountain to the home of his mother, Larcena Hogg, on Kings Creek.

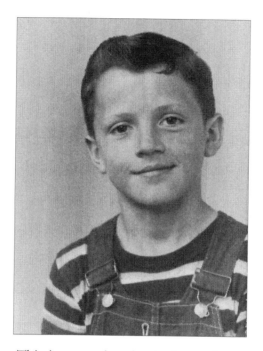

This is my only school picture from my time of attending the schools of Letcher County, Kentucky. I was in the third grade at Lower Kings Creek School, 1947-48.

1 INTRODUCTION

When I die, if I'm judged deserving I hope I'll be permitted to fly back like Ebenezer Scrooge and hover over the village of Roxana, Kentucky and see it as it was during the five years following the end of World War II. It was a time of hardship for my family, but for a child with a thirst to understand what made people tick it was a deep reservoir of possibility. There was much to scratch my head about, a good bit to laugh at, plenty for a grown man to remember and cuss about, and, in the big picture, only a little to cry about. If I luck out and get to take that ghost flight, I might wince to see the hard knocks all over again, and I know I would cry in places, but I'd pay that cost just to see the parts I missed.

· · · · · · · ·

In 1945 I was learning my ABCs at school, and at home I was learning a lot from just sitting on our front porch and paying attention to everything within sight or hearing. I watched it all, not always understanding what it was I was seeing but taking particular note when grownups were laughing loudly or otherwise letting their hair down and arguing, swearing, or fighting, including the time I witnessed a brutal fist fight that ended in a shooting. I watched spellbound from our front porch swing, about a hundred feet from the brawl taking place out beside the L & N railroad track.

This was five years after the death of my school-teacher father at age thirty-one, and as poor as our circumstances were, we could take comfort in the fact that the six of us were still together under one roof. Together, until our trusting and unsophisticated mother came to accept how little it was in her power to keep her family whole.

In the wake of those blows and a few others there came a blessing of sorts; my four older siblings and I had to be fostered out, and that got me out of Roxana. In hindsight, I believe that on balance my removal from Roxana was a good thing, but I didn't feel so thoroughly blessed at the time, not when I found myself far back in the head of a mountain hollow and even farther back in time.

It may not surprise anyone to know that a few years later I was a messed-up kid and prone to act out with cussing and fighting. Now, at seventy-three years of age and a world away from my childhood home beside the L & N Railroad tracks, I look back at the influences: the extremes of behavior; the violence that could flare like a match and almost as quickly die down; the social blend of the unwashed and uneducated rubbing shoulders with the ones striving toward goals; and the cut-and-dried attitudes of the one sort toward the other.

Memories of that hard-fought childhood must have receded from my conscious mind as I took on the adult responsibilities of work and a family of my own, but here in my later years they prod me to look back and reexamine everything I can recall about that turbulent time.

When I was moved from the hills of eastern Kentucky to the city of Lexington, I had a lot to unlearn. My childhood experience of moving and adjusting, or failing to adjust, to confounding new situations might show how adaptable children can be, but the challenge to adapt didn't end when I became an adult. I only had more questions, and late in life the questions are about the places and people of my childhood.

I'm a sucker for 1940s movies, and every time I watch one I am struck by the thought that, my God, we were a half-century behind the times.

Were the people and the local norms as far out of the greater cultural mainstream as was impressed upon my young brain? I'm left to believe that they were and that seeing them through the skeptical eyes of an adult will only show them to have been even more so.

It isn't only out of curiosity that I want to revisit that time; I would hope to gain insight to the life choices—the good, the inconclusive, and the demonstrably poor—that I've made.

I would start out small and work up, taking for my first quest, for example, why it was that at seven years of age I acquired a taste for salt-cured pork in its raw state, straight from the smokehouse, with raw onion, cold cornbread, and a glass of buttermilk. It wasn't for lack of other things to eat. My mother fed me well enough and my diet was about like that of any other child in our village. I had everything I could know to want. I had a mother's love and a slice of soft store-bought "light bread" anytime it suited me to quit whatever game I was playing and come inside, away from the patch of bare dirt that lay between our house and the railroad track.

With some minor misgivings I judge my first six years in our trackside hamlet to be entirely satisfactory. That may be simply the opinion of one who was traumatized to the point of repressing the truth, but I do seem to recall being fairly happy for those very early years. And though I may contradict myself here and there, I still hold to the belief that I fared well enough over the next three years as well, when I lived far back in the headwaters of a lonely hollow, in a place and among a people largely unaffected by events in the outside world. The customs there were so much like Charles Dickens might have described that one could argue that I had gone to live late in the previous century. That cultural time warp accounts for the delay in my discovering America, which in a sense I did, at age ten, in 1949, as I stepped down from the train in Lexington, Kentucky and said to my incredulous self, "Damn, look what I been missing."

A feeling persists that I've lived some longer than seventy-three years. I believe it comes from my having spent those early years in a place where the people kept largely to behaviors of their forebears and carried on with practices that had sustained them for close to two centuries.

From April of 1946 to the summer of 1949 I lived at the head of a remote hollow with an elderly couple who as children themselves had driven teams of oxen to drag great hardwood logs from the old-growth forest. These hardy survivors were little influenced by anything taking place farther away from their shady domain than the general store or the grist mill.

Quaint in their manner of speaking and not at all self-conscious about it, the people of Pace's Branch spoke corruptions of modern English words and a smattering of pure Elizabethan words. They said *Holp* for *Helped*, as in, "He *holp* Pap to milk the cows." In Elizabethan speech *scace* was an adverb that has since come to be replaced by *scarcely*, but on Pace's Branch they said *scace* where outsiders would have said *scarce*. These speech anomalies weren't common to everyone on Pace's Branch, but for Bill and Mary Calihan, who were exceedingly

3

disinterested in the materials and manners of the Twentieth Century, they were the norm.

It's to them, Bill and Mary, that I owe a debt of gratitude, for though I once thought them to be unschooled and simple, they have long stood high in my estimation of their basic goodness and worth. Living with them planted in me a seed that was to grow over the years until I've come to appreciate how rich is the man who has one dollar more than he needs and is comforted by the fact of it.

On a summer day in 1949 I had no realistic notion of the cultural leap I was about to make. My brother and I, each gripping a paper sack filled with our few belongings, lingered on the porch steps and told the sad old couple that we wanted to go live with our mother. That's all we knew or cared about at the time; we knew only that we'd been sent for, that our mother was now living in Lexington, Kentucky, and that at last we'd be with her again.

We could not accept title to the Calihans' little house and their land in exchange for staying on with them. We said goodbye and departed the head of Pace's Branch for Roxana, there to board the L & N Railroad train for a one-way trip to Lexington.

I wasn't too young to notice how adults behaved toward one another and to size them up as "good" people or "bad" people, and most Roxana people were good citizens. It's just that common good manners and law-abiding behavior left no lasting impression on me. I was a child there, and "regular" people, the ones that never frightened or amazed me or who didn't often cause me to laugh, the ones that a more sophisticated observer might have remembered for their laudable deeds, alas, few of them found a sticking place in my memory.

When I think of Roxana I think of a *time* more so than I think of a place. The place is still there but vastly changed from what I remember. Today's Roxana residents can have little more than last names and DNA in common with those who populated the place seventy years ago. Before 1950, we had been isolated, by the limitations of our mountain culture and by poor transportation and the lack of telephones. I was born at the end of the Great Depression and my formative years were during and right after World War II. An economic boom followed the war's end, and returning GIs had seen some of the world, and in no way could Roxana remain what it had been. Still, in the late 1940s I got to see a generous sampling of the unselfconscious behaviors that had led the region as a whole to be caricatured by outsiders. It was as though a depression, and then a war, and then huge advances in technology—automobiles, telephones, television, and better roads—stirred us for a time to hold more firmly to old ways.

Sociologists have described the great population shifts, and the late mountain lawyer and author Harry M. Caudill has told at length how change came to the Kentucky coal fields. No doubt Roxana came through the changes much as any other place in the region did, but I wish to tell about a brief time that now seems to me to have been exceedingly stimulating for a developing young mind. Other outlying precincts surely must have had their characters, the odd, the colorful, and occasionally, the dangerous ones, but I knew nothing of other places. Roxana was my entire world, and while I made no studies *per se* I stored up scenes, events, and characters. I'll leave it to sociologists to debate whether my childhood experience was awful, just average bad, or, despite all the contrary indicators, beneficial over the long haul.

I hope that in the pages ahead I don't go too light on praise for mountain character as I tell of the ways in which my people were different—sometimes lamentably, often commendably—from outsiders. By outsiders, I mean those persons who took sliced bread for granted and wore low-cut shoes in the middle of the working day and whose ignorance on the matter of mountain disputes was evident in their preference for lawsuits over the time-honored practice of settling grievances with fist fights.

Water snake: The fright was worse than the bite.

2 Snakebit from the Start

I was born on Kings Creek in Letcher County, a section of southeast Kentucky's hill country that lies tight against the western tail of Virginia. With my birth we made a family of seven living in a snug little four-room house. My father died before I could remember his face or the sound of his voice, and we remained in the family home but three more years. Of those years I remember little, but I still have a hazy recall of one frightening event. I don't hold much with omens, but this memorable mishap had the makings.

I was a tot of three or four years on the summer day when I followed my four older siblings, two sisters and two brothers, to go wading in the shallow waters of Kings Creek, which flowed along the foot of the far hillside, a stone's throw beyond the unpaved road that fronted our house. Discarded railroad cross ties lay here and there along the creek bed. With the coming of a graded gravel road and the changeover to trucking coal out of Kings Creek's mines, work crews had salvaged some five miles of steel rails and tossed the wooden cross ties hither and about. One such timber lay in the stream bed and I headed for it. Balanced across a submerged rock, the crosstie wobbled as I stepped up on it, and this caused me to step back into the ankle-deep water. The instant that my bare right foot broke the surface of the water, I felt a sting on the outer part of it, and I looked down in a breathless fright to see a spotted water snake wriggling away.

The fang marks were plain to see as the water washed across my foot and carried away thin streaks of blood. My sister, Argyle, almost exactly ten years older than me, took me by the hand and led me screaming back across the road to the house. There she washed the punctures with rubbing alcohol and bound my foot in strips torn from a bed sheet.

I doubt that I possessed even the idea of snakes, much less any notion that one might be poisonous, but I'm sure that my older siblings must have worried, at least a little, that I might die. But there was nothing to be done but wait. Mother was at work, and my father had died three years earlier, in 1940, when I was but eight months old.

One other poignant memory of that time on Kings Creek comes not from my recall of the actual event but from the tale so often retold in later years by one or the other of my siblings, when one of them felt the pull of nostalgia and the need to embrace us all and take us back to a time when circumstances bound us closer than we'd ever be again.

With our mother at work and time heavy on their restless minds, my brothers and sisters, having not one dime among them and no means of getting any place to spend it if they'd had it, made fun from nothing. Their games, made up on the spot, most often involved a challenge or a dare and the risk of physical injury or humiliation. On the day in question, they chose sides and waged war by bombing each other with corn cobs, and if they were soggy corn cobs, so much the better, as the dry ones just floated along and landed with no blood or bruise to be tallied.

We shelled corn to feed our few head of livestock, so there was a never-ending supply of corn cobs. They were cheap ammunition and generally nonlethal, which isn't to say that if properly launched they wouldn't addle the child who doubled back around the corner of the barn and shrieked too late at the sight of a cob-wielding fist raised high to strike from five feet away.

During the cob fight one of the culprits ran across the porch and, just as she passed in front of a window, caught sight of a corn cob flying on a track to brain her. Moments later the intended victim tearfully lamented that she had reflexively ducked and by not taking the sodden cob to the side of her head she was at fault for allowing it to smash through a pane of glass.

A broken window pane meant big trouble, with shouting and whippings. The hardware store in Whitesburg, Kentucky could just as well have been two counties away, since neither we nor any of our neighbors owned an automobile.

With no hope of repairing the damage they'd done and envisioning the red welts that their tender behinds would bear, my four older siblings considered how they might escape punishment for their carelessness, but they found no ready answer. So they prayed. On their knees in the yard and facing the window, they prayed to God to replace the broken pane of glass.

God forbore to answer, but in their extreme anxiety my brothers and sisters clung to hope, and they prayed again and again, and they squinted anxiously between their fingers to see if the miracle had been delivered.

At last it came time to accept blame and face up to their wrongdoing. But wait! Who was it that could have done this deed and yet be forgiven for his error? Why, it was the youngest, the baby of the family, little four-year-old Forester. Too young for a whipping, at worst he'd get a mild scolding, and then Mother would clasp him to her bosom and kiss and comfort him and dry his little tears. It was an inspired solution, and so the perpetrators, tired as they were from all that time on their knees and not knowing how much heavier would become their burden of guilt, breathed a collective sigh of relief.

When Mother arrived home they acted out their infamous drama and allowed as how "Forester's little and he don't have no sense yet, Mother, so please don't whup him." She didn't whip me, of course, because our mother, like most mothers, knew her children. She was then and remained for years to come a human lie detector and a deadly interrogator, and as I grew in years and errant behavior I came to respect her more and more, and to try harder and harder, and fail, to keep from her the foul truth of miscellaneous misdeeds.

I have no memory of my father. His death certificate says he died of pneumonia, but I think pneumonia was just a complication, a follow-up to peritonitis that ensued from a ruptured appendix that was owing to obstacles that stood in the way of timely medical attention. Appendicitis struck him during a visit at the home his father-in-law, all the way at the head of Big Branch, a place reachable only on foot or by horseback. He walked the three or four miles out of Big Branch and on to Roxana where he found motor transport to the hospital in Whitesburg. Relatives quickly lost confidence in the treatment provided there and took him to the hospital in Jenkins, but the peritonitis was beyond reversing, and so he died at age thirty-one, leaving my mother to grieve and to face alone the task of raising five children.

Frightened at the economic peril she faced, my mother held out for a couple of years until she had little choice but to dump the financial burden of the family home and move us to a shotgun shack in Roxana. A shotgun shack is so named because all its rooms line up in a single row with all their doors on the same side of the fragile structure. If you opened all the doors in that place, you could stand on the front porch and fire a shotgun through it and know the pellets would strike nothing until they rattled the leaves of the apple tree out back. Our shotgun shack was all-around shabby and a sorry comedown from our comfortable little house on Kings Creek.

I can recall but little of our life in that house on Kings Creek. My best memories of the old place were to be collected in Roxana, where I first came into some awareness of the world around me. Most of my aunts, uncles, and cousins on my dad's side of the family still lived on Kings Creek, and if Roxana was the locus of our survival, Kings Creek remained our true home.

It was to Kings Creek, to Granny Larce's house, or else to Uncle Isaac and Aunt Gladys's place just off Kings Creek in Lucky Branch, that we repaired for relief from the debasement of living in our Roxana shack that sat just eighty feet from the railroad track. But we had no car, so we didn't often have the pleasure of getting away from Roxana.

I was not much past the toddler stage, so I can't say that I suffered by living in a house that was fit only to feed a ten-minute bonfire. It's only by reflection, with the benefit of accounts told to me later on, that that hovel has brought me any pain, and that's the pain of knowing what my mother and the older ones of my siblings must have felt.

Other than remembering the time my mother fired a shot into the ground to get rid of a drunken lout that threatened violence to me, my only other semi-clear recollection of that decrepit place is one Sunday when Uncle Isaac brought his family to share a chicken dinner with us. Someone caught a chicken and my mother wrung its neck. Then she scalded it and plucked its feathers. Aunt Gladys wadded a brown paper sack, lit it with a kitchen match, and singed off the pin feathers. Next, Mother gutted the chicken and expertly cut it into pieces by hyper-extending the joints and plying a razor-sharp knife across the taut tendons. She stripped the tough yellow lining from the chicken's craw and then made two precise cuts to reveal the three-lobed gizzard that we lovers of chewy dark meat know how to find on the Drive-Thru menu at KFC.

When the chicken platter hit the table, I wanted that gizzard, but Cousin Wade, about the same age as me, allowed as how he liked gizzards too. We fought, which wasn't unusual for us, and I don't remember the outcome, but I expect I had to share that good gristle.

3   Attitudes: Us and Them

In 1945, with six years of life experience, I didn't have a working frame of reference for events that my elders and their friends discussed with seeming great passion. With my limited vocabulary, what they said went sailing off high above my head, all as frustrating to me as trying to make sense of sounds coming from our radio. I snatched from the air only about one in every ten words spoken by the tiny people who hid themselves inside our big battery-powered console radio. By June 19, 1946, however, I had another year of experience behind me as we all listened to the boxing match between Heavyweight Champion Joe Louis and challenger Billy Conn. I finally got the gist of what the radio elves were hoarse from screaming about. This heavyweight championship bout aroused much excitement among the grownups, and we all rooted hard for Louis, even if in our relative social isolation many of us knew little more of black Americans than we did of Bedouins in the Sahara Desert.

I had never remembered seeing a person with black skin until one day, at about age five, I stood transfixed at the sight of a man that I know now had to have been a porter on the L & N railroad's passenger train.

The people of Roxana didn't have to exert themselves to practice segregation of the races, just as they didn't have to work at belonging to a close-knit group that shared the same values. The fixedness of coal mining camps and the natural barriers to travel did the segregating for them. Blacks were so effectively ghettoized in mining camps as to make racial harmony a matter of little consequence to the average white Roxana citizen.

I often overheard two common categories of jokes, those that demeaned blacks and those that demeaned the Irish, jokes about "Rastus an' Liza" and jokes about "These two arsh'men, Pat and Mike". We laughed at Pat and Mike's comical mishaps, but to roundly revile them would have been to revile ourselves, for the story teller was most often ethnically the same as Pat and Mike. Perhaps only in the hills could the tide of Irish immigration that peaked in the mid-nineteenth century have seemed so recent as to countenance these crude jests.

Rastus an' Liza were much safer targets. They stood for an entire race and were treated much less gently than the Irish when it came to the punch line. I trusted my elders, as any young child would, and I never doubted the truth of what they said. So, as I matured I had some way to go to overcome the racial and ethnic stereotypes that were lodged in my developing brain.

Never in my early years was I to hear and remember anyone discuss an actual living, breathing, black person of whom they had any firsthand knowledge. We seldom saw anyone who was, ethnically speaking, from outside our comfortable sphere, but when such a one came our way we laid the hospitality mat on our collective doorstep as at the same time we scrutinized the newcomer for faults attributable to "that type of person".

By the time I came into the world, President Roosevelt's Works Progress Administration (WPA) had already upgraded our county roads and built concrete bridges across every meandering stream that intersected them—in some cases as often as five or more times in a single mile—and the workers had long since departed from the hills. As I walked along the Kings Creek Road to and from school in the fourth grade, I studied what remained of the bore holes in the cliff faces, the smooth vertical grooves that were the back halves of the deep holes drilled by the mostly-Italian road crews. I learned later on that these holes had been filled with dynamite and the rock blasted away, leaving a permanent record of how the way was cleared for the road.

My aunts and uncles were well versed on the highway and railroad construction that had opened up the coalfields for exploitation by the big steel companies and other outside interests. One loudly-opinionated uncle spoke of the WPA and related tales of the "tally wops", who evidently had constituted a significant portion of the WPA workforce. The slur did not seem to me truly mean-spirited, or else I was just too young to sense how dismissive it may have been. I don't know either if real malice was intended when we casually branded outsiders as "bohunks" and "polacks". We had little of the world's wealth to brag about, so perhaps it remained for us to hold firmly to our perceived ethnic superiority. As poor as we were, we were white, and as long as we weren't corrupted by city living, then perhaps, even if we did not occupy the cultural high ground, we could believe that we perched high enough to allow us a downhill view of imported laborers.

If my kinfolks looked down on outsiders and gave them unwanted names, those unflattering names were as benedictions when compared to the undiluted hatred and hellfire that I heard spewed upon foreign leaders who made war against the United States of America. My mother, all my aunts and uncles, my grandparents, they all vented their loathing of Hitler, Mussolini, Tojo, and Stalin, and if any of my hawkish kin were among fellow die-hard republicans, they might dice up that democrat rascal in the Whitehouse, old "Give 'em hell, Harry" S. Truman.

I still love poring over vintage magazines, especially *Look* and *Life*. The photos from World War II reach out to me and I hear their silent stories: the devastation at Pearl Harbor; Gen. George S. Patton, who famously said, "No bastard ever won a war by dying for his country. He won it by making the other poor dumb bastard die for his country."; Gen. Douglas MacArthur, wading ashore at Leyte, in the Philippine Islands, in October of 1944, returning as he'd promised in March of 1942 when he'd fled the Japanese onslaught of Bataan and escaped by PT Boat to Australia; and the iconic images of the average soldier, sailor, and marine are burned in my memory.

The popular press was in the battle, pumping up morale at home. Even the animated cartoons from Hollywood pitched in, dehumanizing the Asian enemy with "Jap" caricatures that featured groundhog-sized upper incisors and squinty eyes behind horn rim glasses in stupidly-grinning yellow faces.

I remember hearing one well-loved aunt speaking of Japanese Prime Minister (Hideki) Tojo in a blustering way that bade ill for old Tojo if she ever got her hands on his yellow hide. He needed a "good killin'".

Certain ones of Roxana's residents were counted on by less well-informed neighbors to give them useful advice and to do it without shaming them. My Aunt Gladys, who tended the small store that supplemented Uncle Isaac's school-teacher income, was always ready to help the customers who laid their problems on the counter. She listened to woeful tales and gave the sort of advice that syndicated newspaper columnists are now paid to dispense. Few knew that she also kept a loaded .32 revolver in a barrel of dried Pinto beans beneath the counter, in preparation for anyone who might come not to make a purchase or seek advice, but solely to make trouble.

My own mother was herself no slouch when it came to defending the domestic premises. I was five years old, and we lived at the time in the shotgun shack in Roxana. I can recall in vivid detail the scene and the action when Mother sent a drunken lout running for cover after he'd brandished a stick of firewood at me.

We had our drunks and layabouts, but they weren't generally dangerous, except to each other whenever three or four dollars were at stake in craps or a poker game. They got reckless when they drank, when their already-weak inhibitions to violence relaxed to where they no longer opposed the violent urge to act now and repent later.

Clyburn H. was such a specimen, a grown man living at home with parents who were themselves just scraping by. Clyburn had a job from time to time, but he usually managed to get fired, once for taking a stick of dynamite from a coal mine explosives shack and sneaking it home in his lunch pail. Besides being a petty thief, Clyburn was a dangerous drunk.

When I was just five years old I didn't know Clyburn, didn't know that he was a man for children to avoid when he was drinking. I learned that lesson one evening when he staggered into our tiny front yard, grabbed a stick of wood off the woodpile, and came on toward me. Just as he raised the club and was ready to brain me, there came the crack of small caliber gunfire, and I turned to see my mother at the edge of our front porch, feet wide apart, holding a still-smoking .22 rifle, the old single-shot bolt-action rifle that had belonged to my late father. She'd placed a round close by Clyburn's feet, and if it didn't sober him up, it got him turned around and headed away from the premises. It was some years later that I came to a full appreciation of the danger I'd been so close to and know that my mother had intervened in a most incisive way, in a way that got quicker results than trying to reason with a drunk.

Why didn't my mother just grab the telephone and call the law? I'm sure she would have, if we'd had a telephone, but to my knowledge Roxana had no telephones in the early 1940s. Which sounds strange to me now as I recall that in the movie *Sergeant York,* which was set during World War I, York's little village in the hills of Tennessee had a telephone. It was the village's only phone, to be sure, but they *had* a telephone—in a store run by Walter Brennan, no less—decades before the telephone was to make a showing in Roxana. The only Roxana telephone I knew about came when my Uncle Steve Whitaker took over the store formerly run by Uncle Isaac and Aunt Gladys and installed a hand-cranked telephone behind the back counter.

Even if my mother had had access to a telephone, it wouldn't have made any difference; the law was at the county seat, Whitesburg, in the person of the High Sheriff, and even if he'd been called and was willing to dispatch help, it was fifteen miles away, too remote to be of any help.

Peace officers worked out of the jail in the county seat. Hamlets like Roxana didn't have so much as a village constable, and this lack of a local peace officer led people like my mother to let it be known in not so subtle ways just how they'd respond to anyone who menaced a member of their family. I've always been proud that my mother didn't hesitate to threaten the life of a normally peaceful man who with no warning became a dangerous drunk.

When one of Roxana's dimwits took umbrage at another of their own kind, they most often spoke with their fists, and sometimes the brawl escalated into a shooting fray. I witnessed one such struggle when we lived in our second Roxana house. We'd recently left the shotgun shack and moved about a hundred yards to a better dwelling, one that had interior walls and separate rooms. A shotgun blast might have passed through the house but not without striking at least one wall.

My mother, as postmistress, ran the Roxana post office out of a front corner room in our new dwelling. I was six years old the day I sat in our front porch swing watching an ugly fist fight between two oafs out beside the railroad track.

An old army surplus ten-wheeler truck sat facing the railroad track. The driver had gone into one of our two stores and left a woman alone in the cab. DJ, a happy-go-lucky roughneck, had moments before been flirting with Nelly D., a young woman who was then boarding with us and helping my mother with household chores. Now DJ stood with a foot propped on the running board and flirted with a woman in the cab of the truck, and he made no move to break it off as the driver returned to inquire, not too timidly, just what the hell DJ thought he was doing. Was he trying to make time with the driver's woman? I don't recall who swung first, but fists started flying and I heard the thuds and smacks. DJ had the best of it until it seemed the driver had

had enough and broke off to return to the cab of his truck. I commenced breathing again.

In a matter of seconds the driver reemerged and put up his dukes. DJ resumed pummeling him, but when it looked as if he would go down, the beaten fellow pulled a small revolver from his pocket and fired twice. All was quiet for a minute as DJ stood with a puzzled look and the driver hustled back into his truck, fired it up, and headed out of Roxana.

We knew DJ and we liked him, everyone did, notwithstanding the fact that he was a brawler and a cad. He was a charming lout, in the physical mold, I'd say, of Clark Gable, even to the sweep of black hair that looped down by one eyebrow.

DJ watched the truck out of sight and then walked calmly over to our porch. He'd been shot through one elbow and had a flesh wound in his side. Nelly D. was wringing her hands and crying, but my mother attended to DJ with great calm, bathing his wounds in alcohol and wrapping them in torn strips from a bed sheet.

If any legal proceedings ensued I never heard any adult speak of them, so I'm reasonably sure that the matter ended on the day it began. Each combatant had acquitted himself in the eyes of his woman; neither had lost face, so what was the need of complex and costly furtherance of the debate? Or, it could have been that DJ was loath to file charges because he didn't want to get on any closer terms with the law than he likely already was.

No doubt DJ enjoyed the attention, and folks couldn't seem to get enough of shaking their heads and saying, "What do you reckon makes him the way he is?" DJ was a favorite topic of gossip, but I suspect some folks secretly admired his reckless ways.

There were others who elicited talk of a more patronizing sort. These were the gallery of unfortunates who could do nothing to change what it was about them that made them objects of curiosity and a perverse sort of pity; humpbacks suffering from spinal curvature that modern medical treatises label *Kyphosis*; *rickets* victims with bowed legs or "pigeon chests" from a lack of Vitamin D; obese persons whose diets likely included all the cheap cuts of pork and nothing from "high on the hog"; the mentally retarded, who were simply "quare" (queer, in the sense of *odd*); the stutterers, and so on, all the ones who endured their afflictions because their families were too poor or too ignorant to seek intervention and treatment.

The less bright citizens always served to exasperate or amuse the acknowledged smart ones, who themselves appeared to show a lack of empathy toward the mentally-challenged but would in extreme cases at least move to see the afflicted citizen transported to the insane asylum in Lexington.

It seemed to me then that we always had at least one village idiot in residence, and if a certifiable idiot wasn't to be found, then an uneducated person with a severe speech impediment would serve as a diversion for the raffish element whose entertainment was where they found it. One such victim was a young woman whose real name I don't remember ever hearing; she was just Bah'r-Wah'r. "Bah'r-wah'r" approximates the sounds she emitted when she tried to make intelligible speech. Seemingly innocent of any knowledge of herself as entertainment, Bah'r-Wah'r was never shy about speaking, or trying to speak. Or, maybe she was as royally pissed off as she had a right to be and was in truth calling the sniggering onlookers every kind of sonofabitch she could think of.

I lacked discernment about what in a person was noble and praiseworthy, and so I confess that my memories are tilted heavily in favor of events that, if taken in isolation from all that would mitigate favorably for a society, would paint a dispiriting picture of the place that was my earliest view upon the world. In my ignorance and immaturity I wasn't measuring the worth of the adults around me, and I imagine that if I'd stayed on in that milieu I'd have acquired the same frame of reference that allowed the majority to take comfort from having been spared the afflictions of others that were so visible in our village. I remember well how freely my elders and betters caricatured their neighbors and friends and certain ones of their own family, with what mirth they saddled them with colorful epithets. Hattie S. had a rump that was "two axe handles wide". So if someone was putting on a little weight, it was "Hey there, Hattie," and if someone stretched the truth to the point of insulting the listener's intelligence, they begged to be held in the same regard as "Big" T (last name/initial omitted), a liar of some renown who nevertheless retained the affection and goodwill of friends and family. As I've said before and am likely to say again, my people, being of limited means, knew better than to muffle anyone whose gift, whether it was spinning tall tales or otherwise causing jaws to drop, was a source of free amusement.

After moving away, as I matured I came to learn of another Roxana than the one I remembered, a Roxana where persons of kind hearts and forward thinking far outnumbered the clowns and misfits. I need no reminders to recall that my great-aunt by marriage, Mahala (Combs) Hogg, had standing as a progressive-minded matriarch. Possessed of dignity and refinement, Aunt "Haley" enjoyed the affection of many and the respect of all. Her adult children far exceeded the local norms for educational and vocational attainment and included teachers and other professionals. Her home, an attractive white frame dwelling, sat on well-tended grounds that featured a lawn that was the equal of any lawn to be found at the homes of Whitesburg lawyers.

Just as we accorded due respect and admiration for Aunt Haley, we felt the same toward Minnie Whitaker, who was also a great-aunt of mine by marriage. A sweet, gentle woman, Minnie, like Aunt Haley, lived a little beyond the Roxana perimeter in the opposite direction from Aunt Haley, in a white frame house with a nice lawn and many flowers and shrubs. Minnie was a superb cook, and I am thankful that long after leaving Letcher County I saw a smiling Aunt Minnie one last time at a family reunion, and I chatted with her and bragged on her dish of fatback-seasoned green beans. I envy my siblings for their having been old enough to appreciate all the good ones at the time we lived among them.

Another unforgettable lady that I have in hindsight come to admire was further down the socio-economic ladder, and all the more to be admired for how well she did, at least most of the time. Bessie W. was quaint even by Roxana standards, a colorful character. She made do pretty well with what she had, and from stories I heard she practiced no deceit about who she was, never complained, and seldom explained. Any story about Bessie would begin with "Bessie, bless her heart," each word inflected with almost-believable sympathy, and if you're from the hills or from the south, you know that "bless her heart" tells you something about both parties, the gossiper and the gossipee. It says, "I know she can't help it, but here's what she went and done, poor thing."

The women in my family would sometimes hire Bessie as temporary domestic help, and one day Bessie was doing laundry and ironing for my Aunt Gladys. Bessie worked in the living space that was at the back of the store. In a corner of the living room, behind the tall *Warm Morning* heating stove, sat a crock jar of fermenting mash, on its way to becoming an alcoholic beverage that's at best a kind of primitive cousin to beer. Bessie caught a whiff, and knowing what was what when it came to home brew, she guessed what was fermenting behind the stove. She didn't waste much time in finding a saucer, the vessel of choice for mountain women to sup their coffee. She dipped the saucer into the crock and supped the sauce. It wasn't many more minutes until her contented humming rose into a full-throated hymn that was full of hope and verging on certainty as pertained to her place in the hereafter.

Aunt Gladys, on seeing that the mash wasn't the only thing that was crocked, guided Bessie back to her house, and they set another time for her to come back and do some more ironing.

I admire Bessie not just because she flouted convention, but because she did the best she could with the little that life had allowed her, and she made few excuses. All of Roxana was invited to the feast that Bessie put on to celebrate her daughter's marriage to a local boy. The main dish was pork neck bones and turnip greens, and all said it was "durn good eatin".

For her individuality, I have to say that Bessie was a Roxana icon, which is saying a lot inasmuch as Roxana had, per capita, more distinctly-different individuals than any other place I've ever lived in.

Roscoe S. also qualifies as an icon. He had a gift, and he shared his gift unstintingly. Every day that the weather permitted I'd see him across the river on his front porch, playing his banjo, and singing, not for himself alone nor just for the dogs under his high porch, but for all and sundry.

Many a summer's evening I'd sit and listen as he twanged his banjo and sang "Ridin' on That New River Train".

> Darling you can't love one
> Darling you can't love one
> You can't love one and have any fun
> Darling you can't love one
>
> Ridin' on that New River train
> Ridin' on that New River train
> That same old train that brought me here
> Is soon gonna carry me home

And so on, frailing his five-string that featured a resonator head of cured groundhog hide, until the final piece of love advice proclaimed the foolishness of trying to love five; "you can't love five and stay alive". That old song is as much a dare as an admonition, just a sly suggestion that, yeah, you can love three or four, and though there may be consequences, they ain't all that scary, not until you try to love five, and that's when you'll wish you'd heeded good advice.

I knew back then that I loved music, but it was only later in my young adulthood, when I'd completed my education and had a growing family and was solid with a steady job, that I found the time to reflect and recall the old songs that lay in the recesses of my mind.

Of the songs I was later to recall so fondly, Ernest Tubb, the first country singer I was to take much note of, scored the most with three that were big hits for him during or right after World War II.

Filipino Baby, a reprisal of a song that was popular during the Spanish-American War.
It's Been so long Darling (but now I'm coming home.)
Soldier's Last Letter (I'm writing this down in a trench, Mom).

Some other songs that come easily to mind are:

Detour - Spade Cooley
Freight Train Boogie - Delmore Brothers
Roly Poly – Bob Wills
Sioux City Sue – Hoosier Hot Shots
Stay a Little Longer – Bob Wills
Smoke! Smoke! Smoke! (That Cigarette) – Tex Williams
Signed Sealed and Delivered – Cowboy Copas

At around 1947 or 1948 I had no notion that Bill Monroe, from Rosine, Kentucky, was making a new kind of music for which he would one day be honored as the "Father of Bluegrass Music". I remember, though, how it thrilled me one evening as I sat on the edge of Uncle Isaac's back porch and heard someone on the radio ripping through a fast banjo breakdown tune. I was hearing for my first time the three-finger style of picking that a young Earl Scruggs, the banjo virtuoso from North Carolina, had only recently introduced to country music fans in the rural South. This wasn't the "frailing" or "claw hammer" banjo sound I was familiar with. The syncopated ringing of individual strings thrilled me down to my toes.

It was an epiphany for me. It was as if in my mother's womb I'd been hard-wired and made ready to hear this music and know at once that I would always need to hear it. Then came the fifties, when I deserted Bluegrass for a space of about five years during which time Little Richard (Penniman), Elvis Presley, Chuck Berry, Carl Perkins, and Jerry Lee Lewis changed everything for me in the world of pop music. Rock 'n Roll maintained its hold on me until in my thirties when I made room again for Bluegrass.

ROXANA

I was thirty years old before I decided I had to learn to play the guitar. I'm self-taught and it shows, but it doesn't limit the enjoyment I get when I mix a Martini and take it and my guitar out on my little patio and play the same songs I've played for many years. It's soul satisfying, even if I sometimes do lament that I left the hills in my early youth, too soon to have picked up a guitar, fiddle, mandolin, or banjo and been tutored by any of the older masters of mountain music whose songs can still today evoke the jigs and ballads brought by their ancestors from the British Isles.

Illustration by Jody

Dropping a rock to explode a railroad torpedo.

4   Roxana

The village of Roxana, Kentucky in the early 1940s had just a few thin-walled frame houses to mark it as any more than a dusty railroad crossing. Most of the houses sat facing toward the tracks of the L & N Railroad. A few yards beyond the tracks the ground dropped off about thirty feet down to the narrow river bed, and at the far side of the river rose a densely wooded mountain ridge.

Sitting on our front porch I could look about seventy yards to my left and see the gray steel truss work of the bridge at the far end of which the road turned sharply left to proceed about five miles to the head of Kings Creek. Motorized traffic crossing the bridge from the far end was generally bound for Whitesburg. On any week day, one or two horses or mules, or an occasional donkey, would come from up Kings Creek and cross the span into Roxana, as those without autos, by far the majority of local citizens, rode in to pick up their mail at the post office and purchase a few staples like corn meal, flour, sugar, twist chewing tobacco, a nickel sack of "jawbreakers" for the kids, and perhaps a sack of nails or some Mason jars for home canning of garden produce.

I am unable to learn the origin of Roxana. I've inquired of the local historical society and I've surfed the World Wide Web, but nowhere can I learn how and when the place was first settled. Until I learn differently I will surmise that it had to do with several nearby creeks and branches that all drained into a relatively short stretch of the North Fork of the Kentucky River. Two of the larger tributaries were Kings Creek and Tolson Creek. Each of these flows through a valley that's two to five miles in length and that has the bottomland to make them desirable places to settle and farm. For a very long time each creek valley had farm residences at intervals of about one-quarter mile. To travel from one creek valley to another meant that one either went across a mountain—a trek that would be arduous if not impossible for a horse-drawn wagon or a sled—or else one traveled along the creek bottom out to the river and then along the river to the mouth of the destination creek.

The distances from Roxana to the head of either creek are close enough to being the same as to make no practical difference. Travel time by horseback was an hour or so in either case. Roxana seems a likely spot for the earliest settlers to have met and traded goods. A store selling dry goods, hand tools, and nonperishable foodstuffs might have been the first business to spring up. Not much else would have been needed by, or within the means of, the farming families, so perhaps Roxana languished with a single store and a one-room post office until coal was discovered in the mountains.

The nation's early industry ran on coal, and the discovery of a vast coal deposit brought the speculators and big steel companies to eastern Kentucky. The lure of money to be made by transporting coal out of the mountains brought the railroad. The extraction and the processing of coal and transporting it to distant cities brought to Roxana and places like it the jobs and commercial opportunities to support more than just a farming population.

Livelihoods changed, but Roxana has continued to serve the same basic purpose, to be a crossroads meeting place. The coming of the railroad and the later construction of graded roads enhanced the commercial possibilities to a degree, but Roxana never grew beyond a few dwellings, one or two general stores, a post office, and at times, a wooden ramp for trucks to drive upon and offload their coal into railroad gondolas.

Roxana was, like so many other crossroad villages, a second-choice sort of place to set down roots and raise a family, and life there could be rough and raw when compared to the generally peaceful existence enjoyed by the creek-dwellers, those families who lived a ways up Tolson or Kings Creek or along any of the smaller tributaries. That's how it was in the 1940s when I was a child and people travelled long distances on foot just to carry out simple errands.

"Simple" surely did not mean "easy", and certainly not for everyday household chores. There was little of Roxana life that was easy. Our kitchen, for example, didn't have a "range" to cook on, but we cooked just the same, after we'd built a coal fire in the cook stove and gotten up enough heat to fry the bacon. Regulating the heat meant closing or opening the damper, a round disc inside the stovepipe that connected the firebox to the chimney. Refrigeration? Just another word that held no useful meaning for us. We had a "smokehouse", but like most everyone else we no longer cured meat by smoking. It was more convenient to salt the pork as a means of preserving it and then hang it in the erstwhile smokehouse.

Although we kept a cow for milking, we never raised a cow for slaughter, and hence, we knew little of beef as a food. A family well off enough to own two cows could make a little money by now and then allowing Bessie or Spot to bear a calf that could be sold for cash. Having a cow bred meant driving it on foot to a neighbor's bull to be inseminated in the age-old and natural way, an occasion that was for me a revelation the first time I witnessed it. I'd previously taken a keen interest in watching our strutting old rooster mount and "tread" the hens in his harem, but I was puzzled as to how the act had anything at all to do with reproduction. I mean, where was his thing? Did he even have one? Now, that bull, he had a thing, a rapier of a thing, and there was no mystery about how he used it on the bellowing object of his ardor. I lost some interest in roosters and was never to find out how they were equipped until years later when I went looking online and learned about something called a *cloaca*.

We kept chickens for the eggs and for the meat, but our favored source of protein was the aforementioned pork. Our only means of having pork was to do it all ourselves; raise the hog and fatten it up, then on a cold fall day that promised frost, to kill the creature and butcher it.

Hog killin' time was a festive time. My uncles and older cousins came along to help. I know now that their jollity was not due solely to the fun of scalding a hog carcass and scraping the bristles from its hide with butcher knives. They invented errands that took them away one at a time and out to the barn, where in the corn crib they'd find a pint of Four Roses. The womenfolk always knew, but they didn't make an issue of it so long as the men didn't disgrace them by drinking openly.

The lack of refrigeration meant that hog killin' took place after fall weather turned cold enough to keep the meat from spoiling before the hams, shoulders, and side meat could be salted and hung in the smokehouse. Which reminds me of a story about an old farmer and the time he caught a ride with a fellow in a new Cadillac car. Sweaty from walking in the heat, he was soon shivering in the cool air that was pouring from the vents of the car's air conditioner. He turns and says, "I believe you can stop and let me out." "You're not going on to town?" inquired the driver. "I was," said the old man, "but since it's turned off cold like, I believe I'll go home and kill hogs."

The hams, shoulders, and "middlings"—our word for side meat—would keep when properly salted, but there was a good deal more to a hog. The woman of the house took charge of the head and boiled it whole to loosen everything from the bone, and then she put this gelatinous mess through a hand-operated grinder. After mixing in pickling spices she poured it all into a container, and as it cooled, the natural collagen content of the meat caused it to gel into a sliceable treat called souse, or, as they call it in more northerly regions, head cheese, or scrapple. Souse by any other name is as tasty as, and doubtless more wholesome than, any processed luncheon meat to be found today in the most renowned of delicatessens.

The lady also took charge of the feet (trotters, to the devotee), which she boiled and then pickled in vinegar and spices and put up in Mason jars. To this day as I pass along the tinned meat aisle of my local grocery store I look longingly at the jars of Hormel Brand Pickled Pigs Feet and sigh because my Cholesterol level won't permit this toothsome delicacy in my diet.

Now we come to the internal organs, and let me first address the one that offered some fun for the kids on Hog Killin' Day, and I'm including here some large "kids" who were known to shave and were rumored to drink "likker" from time to time when no one was watching. The organ I speak of is the bladder, which we inflated and tied off at each end to create what served admirably as a football. It was the right size, if a bit lop-sided, and the walls were nearly as thick as the covering of a regulation pigskin. When kicked, it sprung from the brogan-shod foot in a satisfying way, even if it did wobble like a baseball pitcher's knuckleball. Since it was too round to be thrown with a catchable spiral, the game was simply to kick it, over and over, and from my own perspective, to marvel that something from inside a hog could be so doggone much fun.

I wonder now, knowing that country people have famously claimed to use "every part but the squeal", why I've never heard of a hog's bladder being cooked and served up in some manner. Maybe it's just my ignorance and someone will say to me someday, "Don't you know nothing? My granny sliced the bladder into little triangles, fried 'em up real crisp and served 'em with Piccalilli." Of course, now that I think about it, I've probably been eating hog bladders all my life, in bologna, potted meat, and frankfurters. And that's from someone who *has* seen how sausage is made. I'm grateful for the experience that taught me not to prejudge what might or might not be wholesome and nutritious, and as I say it, it's hard not to feel a little smug about my openness as concerns what is edible. I feel sorry for picky eaters. My kin apparently didn't know about Chit'lins (chitterlings), so they simply discarded the hog guts. I won't search the meat department at Walmart for chit'lins, but I'd give them a try if ever they were set before me.

The liver and kidneys we generally cooked up and served at a big dinner, as we called our mid-day meal, on Hog Killin' day. The long table groaned from all the meat, all the vegetables so recently gathered from the garden, all the pies made from home-grown rhubarb, apples, and cherries, from the big brown biscuits and the steaming cornbread, all of it slathered with home-churned butter. In my large extended family were women who took justifiable pride in the tempting dishes they made without ever consulting written recipes.

With dinner done with and the hog properly butchered, the noble hog, in the mountain way of speaking, "has give an' he's give," but he has yet more to give, and that is the lard and the cracklings. Everything "high on the hog" has been processed, leaving only the jowl meat and the belly meat, the "low on the hog" meat that's too fat for any other use except to be rendered into lard. These lowly parts thus made a valuable contribution, because lard was the only fat available for the frying pan, or to grease a baking sheet, or to shorten (make crumbly or flaky) the dough mix for biscuits and pie crusts.

But the fat meat gave even more, and it did this in a big black kettle that hung above a blazing wood fire. With skin still attached, the hunks sizzled and shrank as they gave up their fat and turned into crunchy tidbits called cracklings. Pork rinds, they're called nowadays when they're packaged and sold in convenience stores. Cracklings were a handy snack, and they also found their way into Cracklin' Bread, a crunchier version of cornbread.

· · · · · · · ·

Recreation for the children of Roxana was whatever we were inspired to do by whatever we found to do it with, and the main rule was "Don't tell nobody". Our parents were responsible adults, and if we'd been foolish enough to tell them of some of our plans we'd have missed out on some memorable thrills. Like the time we set out to see how fast a fodder sled would travel down a steep hillside that was slick with broom sage. Broom Sage Hill, we called it, and for quite a long time we'd been satisfied to go whizzing down it in corrugated paper boxes. A thick stand of broom sage on a steep slope works as well as a layer of grease to reduce friction against a smooth-bottomed conveyance such as a discarded paper box large enough for two or three not-too-closely-supervised children to squat inside and take a swift trip down a hill.

Broom Sage Hill was even steeper for the bottommost one hundred feet or so, for there began the ugly slash in the earth where it had been bulldozed away to accommodate the back portion of Hiram Mitchell's store. The trick was for the rider to bail out of the box where the broom sage ended and the bare dirt began, and then slide on his or her ass until the bare dirt brought them to a gentle stop well short of the weathered boards on the back wall of the store.

The same principle would work for a fodder sled, right? Of course. The sled was a crude wooden box, about five feet wide by ten feet long, with three-foot side panels, all resting upon two runners hewn from tree trunks. When the runners encountered the packed soil at the bottom of the hill, the sled would decelerate and stop short of the store building. It just stood to reason.

In hindsight, we should have tested our theory with crash dummies. But we had no TV, no *Mythbusters* from whom we might have learned the folly of our plan, and so we went fire-in-the-hole and hell-bent the first time out. Six live crash dummies, careening and screaming down Broom Sage Hill, still picking up speed as we slammed into the back of Hiram Mitchell's store with a force that rearranged the merchandise that old Hiram had shelved on the back wall.

We paid in cuts and contusions, and our cash-strapped mother paid Mr. Mitchell for the bottles of rubbing alcohol and sundry liniments and balms that constituted the main wreckage of our adventure.

The L & N Railroad bore the cost of some of our risky fun when we'd occasionally snatch from the tracks a "torpedo" or a "fusee". A torpedo was a flattish explosive device that when strapped to a rail by two bands of soft lead exploded to sound a signal to the engineer up in the cab as he rolled over it. A fusee was like a road flare that a motorist of today might see in the darkness ahead, a brightly glowing warning that a stalled eighteen-wheeler sits on the shoulder of the road. Fusees had a sharp nail at one end, and conductors and brakemen threw them by hand to stick into a crosstie and signal to an approaching train.

Torpedoes were our favorite. Usually an older boy would run out and fetch the torpedo and we'd all head for a little bluff behind our homes, at the top of Broom Sage Hill. There we'd first remove the soft lead straps and save them to make fishing sinkers. We'd then place the torpedo, about the size and shape of a fried egg yolk, on a flat rock at the bottom of the ledge that jutted out from the hillside. Finally we'd all gather on the outcrop above the ledge, and as the rest of us held hands over our ears, the lucky designee, usually the biggest boy, would drop a rock onto the torpedo. With the loud bang echoing in our ears we'd split up and run, knowing that to be caught was to get a whipping. Not a paddling, but a thrashing with a stout switch. After all, what we in our ignorance had stolen from the railroad could have been meant to stop an oncoming train and prevent a deadly collision. We were ignorant of the potential consequences of stealing railroad signals, but we saw them as fireworks of the very best kind, the kind that was free, that were infinitely more dangerous than piddly firecrackers, and that made one helluva bang.

When I say that our parents were responsible, I suppose I mean that they were not so much responsible for telling us what not to do as they were responsible for thrashing us when we in our ignorance "went and done" it. That's how we learned, by doing what we weren't supposed to do and then paying the price of our dangerous diversions.

As noted earlier, my father's brother, Isaac Hogg, and his wife Gladys (Whitaker) owned and operated one of the two Roxana stores. Hiram Mitchell's was the other one. Two stores sitting almost side by side and vying for the limited trade. Each store carried virtually the same line of merchandise: soda pop, candy, cigarettes, crackers, bologna, dry beans, some yard goods, soap, tooth paste, headache remedies, dry cereal, livestock feed, and the like. If Uncle Isaac had an edge it was the gasoline pump that dispensed Gulf gasoline. The customer cranked a handle to pump a measured amount of reddish gasoline into a glass cylinder at the top of the pump, and from there it flowed by gravity into the fill tube of the customer's vehicle. I remember a school-teacher relative, Blanche Hogg, driving up in a new 1948 Ford Sedan. Always smiling and jovial, she'd say, "Fill it up with that Good Gulf," echoing the advertising slogan that one saw in the popular magazines of the day.

I took particular note of the few motor vehicles to be seen in Roxana, but freight trains of the L & N Line awed and fascinated me.

How I wish my child's brain could have absorbed everything there was to know about those steam locomotives. Towing a hundred or more hopper cars laden with coal required the power of a large steam locomotive, and the locomotives we routinely saw were behemoths to my eye, the "eight-wheel-drivers" of song and legend. With eight driver wheels, four to a side, each about five feet in diameter, an engine and its coal tender car stood so large and long it dominated the Roxana scene and seized the attention of every child and many of the adults about.

These monsters were the thrill of my young life, and whenever one sat idling not fifty yards from our front porch, I was bound to stroll out and study it up close. I'd watch the fireman, in his overalls and denim coat and his cloth cap with the narrow stripes, as he went about with a long-spouted oil can squirting it here and there onto what were evidently critical points of lubrication.

The locomotive faced a mighty task to get a "coal drag" rolling forward from a dead stop. Often the big driver wheels would spin in place, spewing a shower of sparks with the connecting rods whipping back and forth before the wheels gained traction on the smooth rails. Sometimes the engineer would pull a lever in the cab and cause sand to spill down onto the rails to improve traction. The sound of taking up slack in the car couplings, from the cab to the caboose that was around the curve and well out of sight, came as brittle clangs that rippled, like a great shiver, up the track, around the curve, and out of sight. The rapid chug-chug-chug like the sound of a muffled Gatling gun would almost stop, and then it would resume with a single chug that sounded like the engine's dying gasp. Suspense hung in the air until at last would come another determined chug, and then, after a pause just a little briefer than the first, the engine would exhale once again, and so on, moving grudgingly faster until the slowly-fading engine sound began to blend with the clicks and clacks of the hopper car wheels rolling over the rail joints in front of where I stood. I'd continue watching until every car had passed by, waiting for the red caboose at the tail end, hoping to see the brakeman lean out from the step and wave his lantern to signal something to the engineer.

Such has been my romance with steam railroading that it was only in my young adulthood that I could imagine train engineers and firemen and brakemen as ordinary humans who lived in houses somewhere and who in their off-the-job time behaved pretty much the same as anybody else.

A train of any sort, if it paused at Roxana, was seized upon by daredevils as a not-to-be-missed opportunity for a stolen thrill ride. Our rowdies were some young men and teen boys who defied parental restraint by being too big to whip or too thick-skulled for counseling. As a freight train or a coal drag lurched into motion, these reckless fellows ran alongside and hitched brief rides by grabbing a climbing rung at the corner of a car and swinging a foot onto the two- or three-step boarding ladder that hung there. With the train gaining speed they'd hang on as long as they dared, and if they waited too long they'd dismount with the intention of running fast enough to stay upright, but often as not they'd go ass over teakettle and come away cut, scraped, and bruised. And laughing, as if it didn't hurt like hell.

I took my own chances once when a train sat idling out on the track. My Cousin Wade and I each climbed up the ladders of adjoining hopper cars and onto a heap of coarsely crushed limestone that may have been destined to be spread between the cross ties and tamped down as ballast to hold them in place. We faced off and began heaving rocks at each other. We generally fought over something every day, so it's likely we were already fightin' mad and were each trying in earnest to brain the other, as we'd let a rock fly and duck for cover behind the steel bulkheads of our respective cars.

Hostilities escalated and we disembarked from the cars, the better to battle at close quarters. Unbeknownst to me, Wade carried an egg-sized rock with him and made to throw it at my head. I tore out toward an old black hearse that sat in front of Hiram Mitchell's Store and round and round the hearse we went, until Wade, the scoundrel, doubled back on me. He'd taken deadly aim and was in mid-throwing motion when, too late, I screeched to a halt and knew I was dead meat. I took Wade's rock squarely between my eyes. It made a gash and a trickle of blood, but inasmuch as it bounced off my skull and left me standing, I choose to remember it as a contest of hard heads in which I was the clear winner.

I was in my late teens by the time the scar, like that of a healed bullet hole, had migrated up into my hairline. Maybe the dent in my skull is normal human physiognomy, but if it is, it's still right where Cousin Wade plunked me with that rock.

I do not wish to leave the impression that my overworked mother wasn't concerned for my safety. She did, after all, have four other children and only one pair of eyes. And no active six-year-old could be kept indoors all the time. I had to be let outdoors, and outdoors was where danger awaited in its many forms; unguarded machinery, rotted porch boards, sparse motor traffic moving when it did without benefit of any sort of traffic management in place, no stop signs, no pavement with painted striping to channel the traffic along recognizable paths; steep slopes and precipices, the occasional shard of glass or jagged-edged lid of a tin can that had been opened by slashing an "X" with a pocket knife and peeling back the four sharp-pointed triangles. And on and on, one danger after another. If the weather wasn't freezing, my bare feet sometimes served as metal detectors, and a trail of blood droplets was as good as a GPS at locating the danger after the fact.

We had been safer at our old home on Kings Creek, where, with the single exception of a Maytag wringer-type washing machine with an engine that ran on gasoline, all our "machines" were hand-powered. We were used to the pitchforks, axes, saws, and shovels. We were practiced in avoiding such snares and pitfalls as there were. Roxana by comparison saw machines and implements come and go, and not infrequently amateurs were at the controls. Occasionally something was left running and unattended, and curious children were bound to investigate. I still feel a twinge of guilt for the time that I and a little friend dropped rocks down the exhaust pipe of an unattended bulldozer. Short of holding the dozer upside down and shaking it, the operator would have had to remove the exhaust manifold to find the cause of the rough idle. If I could today hear the words of the angry bulldozer man, I would grin and bear it as he described the "little heathen bastards" who'd do such a thing.

Mother's attention was continually fractured and sidetracked, and she's not to blame for the time I smashed and blackened a total of eight fingernails, four on each hand. I had a sometime friend, Wilford, who at the time seemed to me much older than he was, when in fact he was just large and at most two years my senior, say, eight years old. Wilford was strong for his age, and his role in our dangerous endeavor of the moment was to haul back on the lever by which a boxcar door was to be lifted slightly whilst I made to slide it open. There was no telling what we might discover, if we could just maneuver the heavy door open and take a peek inside.

Wilford pulled the lever back to about Twelve O'clock but could pull it no farther. Seeing that he required more muscle, I grasped the door in the only way that was available to me, which was with my fingertips under the bottom edge. We strained and grunted and lifted the door from its rusty track, but it was far too heavy for us to shift it laterally. Wilford gave no warning when suddenly he let the handle fly from his grasp, and an anvil fell on my fingertips, or so it seemed for an agonizing few seconds.

I don't know what all I said at that moment, but I think I'd be prostrate with bitter disappointment to learn belatedly that I wasted such an opportunity to yowl the vilest oaths at my considerable command, and damn the consequences, every word and every combination of words, the learning and practice of which had bought me whippings and mouth washings with soap, despite my most inspired excuses, including: "God, well you see, God is God, you see, and, uh, dam, a dam holds back the water, and I guess I just put 'em too close together." Words could not describe the pain, however, and the phrase "flattened distal phalanges" never crossed my young mind, but take it from me, words absolutely do get you past the very worst of it. So, did I swear? Oh, I may have said something like, "Durn you, Wilford. Durn you to perdition," and I may have asked rather too familiarly of the Deity that He send Wilford on a one-way trip to Hell.

I left my swearing at the railroad tracks and my mother mixed soothing words in with her scolding. She soaked my pulsating black fingers in warm bacon fat and wrapped them in the usual way, strips torn from an old bed sheet. (From the way she could rip bed linens into bandage material, my mother might in a previous life have spent some time in a Civil War surgery tent.) Then she sat me in the corner behind the warm cook stove where eight individual fingers were slow to regain sensation in the form of wracking throbs that seemed never to end, and I sobbed myself to sleep.

Brother Jim, at two and a half years older than me, was more knowledgeable of the ways in which our older friends chose to maim themselves. It was at best incomplete knowledge. He knew the steps involved in using carbide[1] to explode a whiskey bottle, but he demonstrated in a most conclusive way that he knew nothing about the all-important matter of when to quit staring at the bottle and fling it away. We stood facing each other at about three feet apart, staring through the amber glass at wispy fumes of acetylene gas rising from a few kernels of wet carbide. Jim was supposed to throw the bottle into the air and have it explode ere it touched earth again, because if the timing was off, the bottle would plop to the ground and just lie there until it exploded in an uninspiring way. He may have been at the point

---

[1] **Calcium carbide** is used in carbide lamps in which water drips on the carbide and the acetylene formed is ignited.

of flinging the bottle when, Blam, it exploded, not two feet from our eyes.

I was miraculously untouched by the glass shrapnel, but carbide, or maybe just the carbide gases, filled my eyes and I was to see nothing again until the following day. Poor Jim took the worst of it as a shard of glass laid the flesh open to the bone on the lower rim of his eye socket. He didn't cry; he just stood there as the blood oozed from the ghastly gash while I did the screaming for both of us.

I don't remember if our mother was apoplectic or if she was calm, but by rights she should have by then been inured to shock at the wounds we inflicted upon ourselves.

We needed transportation to Whitesburg for emergency medical treatment, but there wasn't a car or pickup truck to be seen in all of Roxana. Luckily for us, Uncle Isaac drove a school bus and it stood parked alongside his store. The two families of us piled into the bus and headed for the county seat. We bumped along the gravel road until we came to the black-topped section a few miles out of Whitesburg. That was when I was to realize that we were making a speed far beyond anything I'd ever experienced; I heard someone mention something about "doin' sixty".

I don't remember his name, but old Doc something-or-other stitched up Jim's wound, washed our eyes out with something that neutralized the carbide juices, and dismissed us with some instructions for follow-up care. Everything was calm on the ride home and I enjoyed it all very much. Good memories, actually, to be the focus of so much anxiety and concern and to get a fast ride in a big school bus, a ride that was just for me and Jim.

People sometimes remarked about what an uncomplaining little boy Jim always was. Bah! He was just in shock, from one catastrophe or another. Once, in what was an eminently preventable, or at least avoidable, accident, he ground a ring of meat off an index finger. Across the tracks from our house sat a conveyer of a portable type mounted on two rubber-tired wheels for towing. On this day it was hoisting gravel from a track-side pit up into the bed of a dump truck. A gasoline engine at the base of the conveyer drove a pulley, around which was a steel cable that looped around a similar pulley at the top end. Jim touched his finger to the pulley to track the revolutions. Naturally, his finger failed to keep pace with the pulley and slipped in between it and the taut cable. He may have flinched, but he gave not a peep as his finger made the circuit and came out showing a ring of glistening white bone. Stoical? Not to my way of thinking. I think Jim was just in shock once again, and if he wasn't in shock, he was afraid to make a fuss, afraid he'd catch hell for taking such a foolish risk.

Here I'll mention something more about how we butchered the meat from the hog we killed each fall, as it figures prominently in one more harrowing experience I was to bring on myself. Country folks didn't skin a hog prior to butchering it; the skin was just part of the meat, the part that made the bacon nice and chewy. It posed a choking hazard the likes of which if Jimmy Dean or Bob Evans were dumb enough to ever have put it on the shelves of a Super Walmart, the families of choking victims would have sued them into bankruptcy.

Breakfast was a leisurely meal and never to be rushed. Just talking and chewing, chewing and talking. And chewing, until one dared at last to hope that a sluice of coffee would encourage a gristly mass of bacon, properly masticated with a bite of crusty biscuit, to slide on down the esophagus.

On that otherwise forgettable day it was well after breakfast and I was alone in the kitchen as I hooked a thick slice of bacon for a mid-morning snack. I chewed it—I'm sure I chewed it—but as to whether I'd chewed it enough, the facts will speak for themselves. Would that *I* could have spoken for *myself* and called for help, but, alas, my airway was clogged tight with a wad of bacon rind.

I didn't run from the kitchen; I was too panicked to move. I was slowly suffocating, until finally my mother came from a front room, probably from the small corner room that was the Roxana Post Office. She saw at once what the problem was and wasted no time in improvising a solution. She needed liquid of some sort to thin the gob that had my throat stoppered like a cork in a jug, but we had no running water, no plumbing of any kind, in fact. What we did have was a pail of milk, still warm and topped with frothy foam from having just recently come from our cow, old Pied. It sat waiting to be strained through a cloth to remove the bits of foreign matter that always ended up in the milk, mainly from old Pied's tail as she switched it at flies.

Strained or not, the warm milk was better than nothing, so Mother took up a long-handled dipper and began to pour the milk into me. I don't know if the milk was a life-saving liquefier or if Mother jammed a forefinger down my throat and hooked it around the wad; I only know that she saved my life. I don't know the extent to which I may have been traumatized by my near-death experience, but I'm right certain that I was thereafter one of the best little chewers my mother had ever seen.

It hadn't been long after my father's burial in the family cemetery that our financial circumstances required us to leave our Kings Creek home and move into the shotgun shack in Roxana. To call the new place substandard would be to heap praise upon such a blighted hovel. It kept the weather outside, but for a family dwelling it failed on all other counts with the possible exception of affordability. Someone should have paid us just for the modest degree to which we kept the vermin out.

One Sunday morning Mother went to attend a funeral at a home on Mill Branch, a couple of miles from home, and left me and Jim in the care of our two older sisters and our oldest brother, Manfred. We were in the sweltering Dog Days of late summer and the Jar Flies' drone coming from the trees beyond the river only made Roxana seem the quieter. No one stirred. Jim and I, limited as we were to playthings of our own contrivance and that cost nothing from anyone's pocket, weren't easily bored, but today we fidgeted and teased out on the front porch.

Jim, who later in high school and college was a standout athlete, especially in track, decided today to find out how far he could leap from a flat-footed start. He made a good show of it. Until it came to landing, and that's when his right leg went crashing through a rotted plank, all the way down through the porch to his upper thigh. And there he remained for a little while, ashen-faced but giving no other sign that a protruding rusty nail had ripped a deep gash four or five inches long into his thigh.

We didn't expect Mother to return anytime soon. We knew funerals were drawn-out affairs where two or more preachers tag-teamed each other to keep up their sing-song, gasping style of preaching, in which these called-but-not-generally-ordained preachers might quote scripture now and then, but they mostly exhorted the listener to repent, to "get right with God". They'd be sure to keep it up until the last sweat-dripping one of them had given his all and was near to collapsing. Someone would have to go fetch Mother away from that funeral, or else Jim might just bleed to death. Older brother Manfred was the strongest of us, so it was he who ran the entire way to the home up Mill Branch and told Mother what had happened to Jim.

In the meantime, and I don't know how it came to be, but an old woman, Granny H., happened by. Granny H. was said to claim some mysterious power for healing, but we all knew she was a witch, a witch who wouldn't harm you if you'd never blackguarded[2] her, for which she'd surely cast a spell upon you.

What I recall learning of that day is that Granny H. washed the wound out with coal oil, and then, in a move that confirmed for us that she was truly a witch, she licked a forefinger and scribed an invisible line around the wound, and lastly she bound it up with the standard wrap, the tried and true strips of old bed sheet. I'm sure that when she arrived home Mother must have rendered first aid that didn't rely on witchcraft, but there was little she could do beyond cleaning the wound and wrapping it as best she could. Of course, Jim would have benefited by being stitched up by a professional, but professional suturing would cost money, and we didn't have money. And besides, nothing was broken, and Jim was a first class healer. One of his thighs, I forget which, still bears a long shiny, parchment-looking scar.

---

[2] **Blackguard:** In Roxana parlance, to blackguard was to disparage someone behind their back, usually by calling them names, especially sonofabitch.

My mother, Chelsea (Whitaker) Hogg, and me. The
year is 1943, war is raging on the other side of the
world, and in my army uniform I'm showing my
(mother's) support for our men and women who are
in harm's way.

5   Junk Food and Quack Cures

Roxana's families ate five basic types of food: cornbread and biscuits, garden produce, home-butchered meat, small varieties of wild game such as rabbits and squirrels, and store-bought treats that we would never have demeaned as "junk food". Moon Pies and RC Colas weren't junk food, and neither was a chilled bottle of Dr. Pepper into which we would almost always upend a nickel bag of salted peanuts.

We didn't have an Italian bakery on the corner, even if we'd had a corner to put one on, and the nearest soda shop was at Quillen Drug Store in Whitesburg, which at fifteen miles away could as well have been on the moon. What we had, and were well enough satisfied with, were the packaged items that wouldn't go entirely bad if they sat for months on the shelves of Hiram Mitchell's store.

I doubt that we suffered much ill effects from all the fat and cholesterol we consumed; our home-grown vegetables may have balanced it all out some, and few of us lacked for exercise. We didn't live on Vienna sausage (vie-ainie, we called it) and soda crackers, but we favored that combo as a snack, that and "potted meat", and sardines, anything, pretty much, that one could layer on a cracker and eat in the same place it was purchased. Usually a fellow would buy a quarter pound box of saltines and sit on a nail keg there in the store and eat what he'd bought. I say fellow, but women sometimes partook.

Snacks like those were almost always followed by a leisurely smoke. It was usually Camels or Luckies, but sometimes it was a small sack of

Bull Durham or a tin of Prince Albert that a man took from the bib pocket of his overalls and sprinkled onto a rolling paper and licked into a passably firm cigarette. The smoker would swipe a kitchen match on a seam of his overalls, pause a few seconds for the sulfur fumes to die away, and then fire up his fag. He'd take a deep first drag, hold it deep in his lungs a few seconds before allowing the smoke to billow out through his nostrils, and then he'd cough and spit, and if his aim was good he'd hit the sand box in which sat the pot-bellied stove, the sand being under the stove to catch the occasional ember that might otherwise ignite the highly-flammable oiled pine flooring.

Amber-colored twisted strips of sticky fly paper hung here and there from the stamped tin ceiling. On the screen door whose grab handle advertised Mel-o-Toast Bread was a wad of cotton that was secured by needle and thread and saturated with DDT as a further remedy for the bothersome flies.

Mitchell's Store sold Lydia Pinkham's Tonic, with 18 percent alcohol, and other herbal remedies, but Lightning Hot Drops was the remedy I heard the most talk about. That could be because it was 60 percent alcohol and had 48 drops of chloroform to the ounce.

Hadacol[3] was another famous elixir back then. Heavily advertised on the radio, Hadacol, it turns out, was much like that "good old mountain dew", and them that refused it *were* few, especially in our ostensibly dry County. I know now why a young cousin perked up so well when his mommy plied him with Hadacol. He was buzzed from the alcohol that was 12 percent of Hadacol's content, which according to the manufacturer was there "purely as a preservative".

All these elixirs and ointments were just one category of mail-order goods that radio stations like WCKY in Cincinnati hawked on hillbilly music shows beamed toward Kentucky. Other items included Rock-of-Ages Brand tombstones and baby chicks with the disclaimer, "No particular sex or breed guaranteed".

With alcohol-laced tonics, in our dry county even the foot-washing Baptists could avail themselves of these curatives without fear of censure.

---

[3] **Hadacol** was the creation of Dudley J. LeBlanc (1894–1971). LeBlanc served a few terms in the Louisiana state Senate, but he was not a medical man. He was, however, a talented salesman who evidently knew the power of radio advertising at the time.

On the topic of foot-washing Baptists, a close relative of mine on my mother's side was a devout foot-washing Baptist with many sons, one of whom was for all his life a renowned prankster. His daddy was a stern authoritarian figure who lived by a verse in Proverbs that says regarding the disciplining of a child, "If you beat him with a rod, he will not die." The daddy was of the Old Regular Baptist persuasion, and he was a deacon of his church. On the eve of a Sunday when the daddy was to be the washee in a ritual foot washing, his son had a flash of wicked inspiration. If he stashed a little soot in the toes of his pa's socks it would be funny as hell when Pa peeled them off in front of the congregation. The mad prankster took the clean socks his momma had laid out and went to the fireplace where he reached up inside the flue and scraped off a handful of soot for each sock.

Would that the prank had played out as the prankster son had planned, for it would have made a better story. But it didn't turn out that way, and the devilish son didn't get the hide whipped off his back. Fortunately for him, but so unfortunately for we who love a good tale, his momma discovered the treachery and without a word to her church-bound husband replaced the sooty socks with a clean pair. It saddens me to think of how one meddling momma thwarted the designs of such a brilliant young mind. Had she but conquered her squeamishness, she'd have realized that bloody stripes on a young back would heal in time but the story would live on in family lore.

Circa 1910: My paternal grandfather, Stephen Lowell Hogg, holds my father, Hobson, while my grandmother Larcena holds younger brother Isaac. After the untimely passing of my father, Uncle Isaac, an all-around good man, became for me a beloved guiding hand.

Circa 1928: My granny, Larcena (Mitchell) Hogg, stirring freshly-churned butter to rid it of excess moisture. Widowed at a relatively young age, Granny was durable and independent and well up to the task of keeping the old farm going.

Granny was armed and ready for any nighttime disturbance.

6   Granny Larce's Forty-Some-Odd

In 1943 my paternal grandmother, Larcena (Mitchell) Hogg, whom we children called "Granny Larce", lived alone on Kings Creek in the next house up the road from my family. She'd borne eleven children, ten sons and a daughter, by her husband, Stephen, and had now outlived him and eight of their children. Daughter Lucinda died at age eighteen. One son died from a shotgun accident while hunting, one by auto accident, and one fell to his death from scaffolding in a Baltimore shipyard during World War II. My father, Hobson, was one of three sons who died from more-or-less natural but preventable causes; in one case it was food poisoning that was laid to a tin of Vienna sausages that a grocer had previously opened and then returned to the shelf. In my father's case, it was peritonitis from a ruptured appendix when he was miles away from motor transport that might have gotten him to a hospital in time.

Granny's house sat on the same side of the road as ours, the side with the most level ground in the creek bottom. The watershed called Kings Creek was not as wide as a river valley nor nearly so closed in as a branch; it fell in the middle. It was wide enough to accommodate the stream itself plus a two-lane gravel road and, here and there, an elongated triangular field. Some of these fields were wide enough for thirty rows of corn, but many more could accommodate only twenty or fewer rows; each row was shorter than the previous as the two enclosing mountain ridges encroached on the bottomland in a meandering way.

The gravel road lay just a few yards in front of our respective houses. It ran from Roxana, where Kings Creek flowed into the North Fork of the Kentucky River, to the head of Kings Creek, where it dead-ended.

Just beyond the dust-laden milkweeds that marked the far shoulder of the road lay the neglected narrow-gauge railroad bed whose steel rails had been taken up when dump trucks became the means of getting Kings Creek coal to the various train-loading facilities.

I never saw it for myself, as it happened before my time, but I later marveled at the singular genius and chutzpah of a man who ran his old dump truck on the train tracks for a while. Willard W., however plain he may have lived, was a resourceful fellow. He took the tires off of his truck and ran it on the rims along the track, grinding and grating but getting coal to his customers without the risk of bald tires going flat. This was one of many events that I never witnessed firsthand but which were the subject of eagerly-told and oft-repeated tales later on in my life.

Little enough light shone into Granny's place by day, and gloom came before supper time as a mountain ridge blocked the setting sun. Roosevelt's New Deal and the Rural Electric Cooperative Corporation (RECC) brought artificial light to other places many years before it got around to Kings Creek. Nights of my early childhood were long, and since Granny lived alone, sometimes one of my older siblings would stay with her, to help her feed the livestock and do the milking and to keep her company at night. So it was that brother Jim, at about age six, went one summer evening to be with Granny.

They completed the evening chores, the feeding and milking, and the sun's fading glow had fallen behind the crest of the east-facing hillside. Granny and Jim took right away to their soft featherbeds and were soon sound asleep. It was time for mice to scrabble along the interior walls, between the blue boards that showed into the rooms and the ancient hand-hewn poplar logs hidden behind the planking. A time for owls to awaken and seek out the small rodents of the fields and fence rows, for foxes to prowl the land, for raccoons to ransack the unsecured stores of human food, for rodents to pillage the smokehouse and the corn crib.

In the middle of the night came Granny's shout of alarm, loud and quavering, "Lord, honey wake up!" Jim, quaking with the certainty that death loomed in the darkness, answered Granny's unnerving summons by bolting half asleep from his bed. "Lordy, child," Granny exclaimed in a tremulous voice, "get me my forty-some-odd. They's a fox is in the henhouse."

Jim hopped to it and fetched Granny's heavy old pistol, her "forty-some-odd". Granny never could remember what was the caliber of her old Colt hog-leg revolver, just that it was a forty-something. She kept it loaded for when the need might arise, and she slept with it under her pillow. On this night, however, she shared the same room with Jim lest he be alone and afraid, while her pistol was under the pillow of the bed in what was her customary sleeping room.

Loud cackling and squawking came from the direction of the henhouse, out in back of the main house, up near the orchard fence. Ankle deep in dried chicken droppings, the air inside choking-thick with poultry mites, the little shelter housed a chicken roost, a homely lattice contraption made from a half dozen thin saplings lashed between two stouter specimens of the same and leaned against the back wall.

When darkness neared, certain ones of the hens disdained the henhouse and chose instead to fly up into the low branches of a tree and there to lock their feet to a limb, tuck their head beneath a wing, and await the rooster's crow that announced the coming of the dawn. With those hens at risk in case of rain, Granny thought it best to leave open at all times a small trapdoor into the henhouse. A fox in the henhouse was a risk she had weighed and accepted.

Where chickens go foxes are wont to follow, and there to snatch a sleeping fowl by the neck and make off into the night. And where foxes can go, or where Granny supposed one might have gone, that's approximately where she'd point her forty-some-odd and let go with a couple of booming rounds. This night she padded barefoot out to the porch in her long flannel gown and her white hair in a long plait. There she raised the heavy pistol with both hands and fired into the cornfield that began at the edge of her yard. I believe my aged granny meant her noisy message for more than just a marauding fox. When the tale got around it might discourage some would-be marauder of the two-legged variety.

On another occasion Granny was more forthright in letting it be known what would be the consequence of wronging anyone, or anything, dear to her. She kept a German Shepherd, Old Jack. My Uncle Doyle Hogg, when he was Sheriff of Letcher County, gave the dog to Granny for her protection, and Granny set great store by Old

Jack. Nobody messed with Old Jack, even if the occasional passerby felt menaced more than was strictly called for when all they were doing was walking the near side of the dusty road as they passed in front of the house.

One day Old Jack barked and growled threateningly at an old woman from up the creek as she walked past Granny's place. Affronted but unafraid, the distant neighbor, with whom Granny was on limited speaking terms that had remained frosty over some long-past slight, planted herself firmly at the gate that separated her from the frenzied dog, and she called loudly, "Larce Hogg, I'm gonna kill this nasty beast if you don't shut him up."

Kill Old Jack? Fightin' words those were, in a place where people didn't hint around about what provoked them but got it off their chest with an economy of words. "Wait right there, honey," Granny called out and left the porch to return promptly with her Peacemaker, her forty-some-odd.

"Oh lordy, Larce, don't shoot me," pleaded the old woman at the gate, "I wun't gonna hurt yore dog. I didn't mean it." Satisfied that she'd made her point, Granny laid the pistol aside and stood, arms akimbo, all five feet of her in her plain cotton dress and apron, with not one bit of color upon either article. Squat and round, her white hair in a long plait, she remained the pale picket on the ramparts and watched until her old foe walked on past the corn patch and disappeared beyond the waving corn tassels.

Indomitable, her habits and predilections shaped by privation and hard choices that were life's portion for a mountain widow, Granny was in all respects a hardy and resourceful survivor. Larcena Mitchell was fifteen years old when she married Stephen Lowell Hogg, a man twenty-seven years her senior. He brought seven children from his first marriage—three of the ten children by first wife Millie had died quite young—and Larcena bore him eleven more, including the second to the youngest of that brood, my father, Hobson Hogg.

My Grandpa Stephen Lowell Hogg—born 1845, died 1923—served in the Civil War with Company B, 13th Kentucky Cavalry, CSA. I can't say what his political leanings may have otherwise been, but he was a subsistence farmer, and being only seventeen years old at the time of President Lincoln's Emancipation Proclamation, it seems unlikely that he would, or could, have owned slaves.

The main reason, though, why I think Stephen Lowell Hogg never owned a slave is the information given for Letcher County in the 1860

Federal Census and in the 1860 Slave Schedule. My Grandpa Stephen was fourteen years of age in 1860 and lived at home with his mother and father. Another man of the same name was forty-six in 1860. This latter Stephen was the head of a large family and quite well-to-do, with real estate valued at $2,000 and a personal estate valued at $7,175, impressive numbers for a Letcher County farmer of that time. I think he, and not my grandpa, must be the same forty-six-year-old Stephen Hogg shown on the Slave Schedule as owning seven slaves and three slave houses.

If the opportunity had come, Grandpa Stephen might well have been pleased to inherit the slaves that belonged to his daddy, Kelly Hogg. But that opportunity never came; it was preempted by President Lincoln's Emancipation Proclamation. So, yes, my great-granddaddy, Kelly Hogg, owned five slaves in 1860, but I'm satisfied that my Grandpa Stephen never owned a slave, however much he may have countenanced slave-ownership by white masters. Regardless of what the truth of that may have been, Stephen returned home after the war to the life of a simple farmer, and one way or another, a farmer had to have many able bodies for all the drudge work involved in making a serious go at living on the proceeds of primitive husbandry. And perhaps that need drove him to sire a total of twenty-one children, ten by first wife Emily "Millie" Stamper, and eleven by second wife, Larcena Mitchell.

Stephen's first wife, Millie Stamper, died in June of 1888, and just four months later, in October of 1888, Stephen, who was then serving a term as Letcher County Judge, married fifteen-year-old Larcena Mitchell. The story that's passed down through the years claims that Stephen, with an ailing wife not long for the world, figured wisely that with a house full of children he'd soon be needing a new helpmeet. Against the coming need for a new wife, Stephen persuaded Larcena's parents to keep her on hand for him and away from temptation and the attention of other suitors.

Stephen was direct in seeking the hand of young Larcena Mitchell in marriage. At the appointed time, he rode to the Mitchell home, which was close by his own home, and was invited into the parlor. There Larcena's papa said, "Judge Hogg, what brings you out today?"

"Well," said the judge, "I think the time has come for me to marry your Larcena." The father thought about it for a minute and said, "Well, all right then." When the judge had departed, shy Larcena, who'd remained in a back room until Stephen had gone from the house, came into the parlor and asked of her papa, "What did Judge Hogg want?" Her papa told her that the judge wanted to marry her, whereupon Larcena nodded in a matter of fact way to indicate that she had no objection.

Mountain social customs, predicated upon need more than stylish notions of what was proper, doubtless allowed Stephen to shorten the period of mourning after his Millie died.

As for Stephen Hogg's judgeship, I think it's noteworthy that he won election to that office by a single vote, an outcome that was owing to the fact that his opponent, Shade Combs, had as a matter of courtesy voted for Stephen.

Stephen's reasons for wanting the judgeship may have been noble, and it isn't for me to conjecture, but needing a source of cash money must have weighed in his decision to serve the citizens of Letcher County. He was a subsistence farmer, owning livestock for the work they could do or for the milk or meat they would make, and growing crops to feed the livestock. These efforts kept the wolf from the door, but they produced little in the way of cash income.

Bartering covered some needs, but with so many mouths to feed, certain necessities had to be bought with cash. He took corn to the mill to be ground into meal to make cornbread, a staple of the mountain diet, and at the local store, he swapped eggs for flour, and so forth, but that left sugar and several other kitchen needs to be purchased.

Larcena sewed, as did any wife and mother of the time whose good fortune it was to own a pedal-operated Singer sewing machine, but fabric to make into everyday clothing wasn't one of the items she bought at the store. Why spend good money on yard goods when the cloth feed sacks of the day constituted a steady supply of gaily-printed material?

But feed sacks didn't suffice for clothing a boy, and the storekeeper required cash for ready-made goods. (My granny referred to all such articles as "brought on".) Getting cash meant that Grandpa Steve had to sell something. Perhaps it was a pig. When the old sow dropped a litter, he kept aside some to fatten and slaughter and sold the others of the litter. Or it might have been that he raised a cash crop. Hemp was such a crop in the hills back in those days, and on up until after World War II it was raised for the fiber that could be made into rope.

Hemp back then was not the *Cannabis* of today, as it had little of the psychoactive ingredient THC, so I doubt that "Reefer Madness" was much in evidence around the old farm. Had my dad and his brothers been toking on weed, though, it might help explain some of the extreme pranks they pulled off.

Organized recreation was a notion foreign to them. Their free time, the little of it that there was, was filled with homemade fun, which often as not began with a dare, or as was the case in one oft-told tale, an idle comment that caught fire in the minds of four bored adolescents.

On certain Sundays, when the monthly church meeting, an all-day affair, had rotated back around to a schoolhouse that was close enough to reach by horseback, the parents sometimes saddled up and rode to the meeting. The boys stayed home, partly because there were only two horses and it was a long journey on foot, but mostly because they didn't have any "church meetin'" clothes—there was a photograph, a tintype pastel, in which the youngest child, my Uncle Isaac, was strategically placed behind a short bushy plant so that his bare feet wouldn't be in the picture. Few families would waste money to have their children shod in the summertime, and not many would dress a dozen of them in Sunday clothes and drag them to an all-day preachin'.

A house full of unsupervised boys, what mischief could they get into, anyway? Pa had wisely left them a list of chores to carry out. He'd delivered his practiced lecture the same as always when he left the boys alone at home, ending with a stern warning not to take the old shotgun out of the house, still, he'd have to admit later that he'd not said a word concerning what they might not bring *into* the house.

Well after the parents had gone on their way to hear the all-day preachin', one of the boys spied a man coming up the road toward the house, a man they all knew and held some resentment toward. Perhaps he'd ratted them out for some earlier transgression, or maybe he'd simply berated them in person, as was the due of one's elders back then, even if they weren't kin.

The boys knew better than to sass an adult, and this adult was a man that had some business dealing with their daddy. It galled them to think they'd have to be polite to the old buzzard. He might stop in, and he might not. It was best to be prepared.

It took them some doing to prepare their greeting, but they achieved ready-and-waiting a little before they heard steps coming along the wide front porch. A knock sounded upon the thick wood door, and the delegated greeter was coaxed toward it. Uncle Isaac was the smallest of the boys and it was his job to squat down and pull the door open and then to remain hidden behind it. Uncle Burnett had the deepest voice so it fell to him to conceal himself and pitch his voice as low as possible and say, "Howdy", as the stupefied visitor stared into the long solemn face of their daddy's old mule.

7   Baby to Angel

First grade babies
Second grade tots
Third grade angels
Fourth grade snots
Fifth grade peaches
Sixth grade plums
And all the rest are
Dirty Bums!

I'd be starting the primer (rhymes with "skimmer"), which is what we called kindergarten, a station below even the first grade babies, and unworthy of mention in a hand-clapping rhyme. "Feckless fetuses" sounds harsh, so maybe I was a "minor annoyance".

New bib overalls, that's what I recall most about my first day at Mill Branch School in the late summer of 1944. Stiff with sizing, my shiny blue overalls had room for growth. In a year or so all I'd have to do was unroll the generous cuff that broke now over my high-topped brogan shoes. The newly exposed strip of fresh denim down by my ankles would be noticeably darker than the rest of my overalls, while the patches on the knees, having been salvaged from a pair of worn out overalls, would be almost white.

Brogans (say it like "brogue Anne's") was what we called our high-topped shoes that had eyelets partway up and hooks for the top three or four crossings of the laces. "Brogans" originally named the highly affordable shoes worn by the Irish working class. They fit loosely either foot until well broken in. My shoes were of a better design in that one shoe was made for the left foot and the other fit only the right foot. They took some breaking in, but after a week or so, they fit very comfortably.

It was still warm weather for me to be wearing a plaid cotton flannel shirt, but neither I nor any child of my acquaintance had any notion of a seasonal wardrobe. And it would have only been natural if I was smarting from a fresh haircut for that first day of school. Smarting, because even though my mother wielded her hand clippers with practiced skill, for every hair that was caught up and cleanly cut another hair resisted cutting, and I felt the pain as the follicle struggled to maintain its grip on my scalp.

I walked along a half mile of dirt road beside the L & N railroad track to where Mill Branch, a stream that ran ankle deep until a freshet hit and washed out anything in its path, emptied into the North Fork of the Kentucky River. After a right turn into the mouth of Mill Branch I walked another few hundred yards along a narrow path to the two-room clapboard school house.

The pale gray structure, backed up as it was to a densely wooded hillside and fronted by a half acre of hard packed bare dirt that ended at the water's edge, resembled dozens of other two-room structures that Letcher County located every few miles along the creeks and hollows so as to be reachable by foot travel. School buses were for hauling high school kids to the school "on the hill" in Whitesburg. For kindergarten through eighth grade, everyone walked.

The floor joists of the Mill Branch school house rested upon stone pilings that bore the marks of the hand chisels that had shaped them. If Mill Branch overflowed its banks, the flood waters just washed among the underpinnings without causing any damage.

Oiled pine planks made for a sticky floor, and on the walls the tongue-and-groove pine wainscoting oozed rosin in the heating season. Large light fixtures hung from the ceiling on long chains. In one corner of each of the two rooms sat a pot-bellied stove. Older students rotated the job of building and tending fires in the stove, splitting kindling wood and carrying coal from the outside bin.

I was taught that first year by my Aunt Evalee, a young raven-haired beauty who was a younger half-sister to my mother. I recall her demonstrating how to make the cursive letter *a* by describing the route a bunny rabbit took as he left the nest and meandered about. First, he scouted to the west and then south-eastward and this scribed the left-side arc of the letter. Next, he scampered straight northward to his home, only to set out to the south again for a short way until he looped toward the northeast and came to a stop. There he sat, and we weren't to learn why he was content to do so until Aunt Evalee got around to telling us how to connect cursive letters.

The playground at Mill Branch was where I learned to tie my shoe laces. I was a five-year-old, after all, and I suppose tying a bow challenged most kids of my age. A kind-hearted classmate, Tommy, made a lasting memory by taking the time to instruct me.

Aunt Evalee must have done a superb teaching job, because at the end of the following school year, as I exited the first grade, another well-remembered teacher, Anna Stewart, certified me ready for the third grade. No second grade tot, not me, and, *hallelujah*, I was one year closer to becoming a fourth grade snot, or so it seemed.

At the beginning of the next school year I wasn't told why I'd be attending a different school. I didn't know why our mother, who was by herself feeding and caring for five children on the wages of a country postmistress, was compelled to board her brood out during what was a lengthy detour on her way to finding a more secure existence for all of us.

I was bound for Granddaddy Jim Whitaker's house on Big branch, where another of my mother's pretty half-sisters would be my teacher.

!939:   At the James Whitaker home at the head of Big Branch.
Family and guests gather to celebrate Granddaddy Jim's 52nd
birthday.   Seated front row, right, are my maternal great-
grandparents, George and Susan (Combs) Whitaker. Second row,
left, wearing a hat, is my grandfather James Whitaker. In front of
him, wearing a white dress, is my grandmother Cannie (Ison)
Whitaker. The others are James and Cannie's children and their
spouses and children. On the porch to the extreme left is my father
Hobson Hogg. He's restraining a friend with a rope so the friend
won't beat him to the long table that's set up outdoors for the
birthday feast.

8   Big Branch

Before Jim and I were farmed out to the Calihan's of Pace's Branch, I spent most of my third school year with our maternal granddaddy, Jim Whitaker, and his wife, Grandma Cannie, as we called her, in their house at the head of Big Branch. Brother Jim spent that year in Whitesburg at the home of a kind-hearted Whitaker uncle. I was six and Jim was eight, in the third and fourth grades, respectively, but that is a guess, since with all the moving around and changing schools I can't be sure what grade I was in while living at any of the several different places I called home after first leaving Roxana.

I didn't know then, and I remain uninformed today, as to the precise nature of our mother's problems that lead her to find temporary homes for her children, but the undeniable facts were these. She was a young widow with five children; she had little or no money, no equity in anything except some household furnishings, no life insurance proceeds from the death of her husband; and with only limited formal education in a meager job market, she had poor employment prospects. I don't know that there were any public welfare agencies she could have turned to. She must have been under a crushing burden of fear and anxiety when she took what she likely saw as the only course open to her and sought the aid of her extended family, none of whom were flush with money but all of whom shared a strong family bond.

Thus it was that someone, I don't remember who, came on foot to Roxana to fetch me. We followed the river course to the mouth of

Tolson Creek, which despite its title of "creek" was a hollow not much wider than the "branch" hollows. The "road" was passable only by an occasional war-surplus Jeep, or by the only machine that was and always will be superior to a four-wheel-drive, a large mule. "Stubborn as a mule" is a saying that unfairly maligns a good mule. Put him in his leather harness and pound-for-pound he'll out-pull just about anything. If a Jeep had as many gears as a good mule, it wouldn't be able to move the weight of its own transmission. I digress, but only because I have some fondness for mules; they're so strong and so willing to do what's asked of them.

Anyway, we walked along by Tolson Creek to the mouth of Big Branch and thence to the last house up that narrow hollow. Granddaddy designed and built his own house. I've seen a bill of sale, dated 1917, for the building materials he had shipped by rail from Lexington to Roxana and then hauled the rest of the way in a wagon over the bone-jarring rocks in the streambed.

It was a handsome white weatherboard house, large by local standards, grand, one might say given the location. It sat at the foot of a steep mountain spur that was densely forested with oak, maple, and hickory. Granddaddy Jim had chosen well his building site, a piece of flat ground that was a geological anomaly for its exceptional size at the head of a mountain hollow. The pie-shaped bottom-land was bounded by two shallow, rocky streams, each flowing from a convergence of rills hidden in the hilly backdrop.

In memory it's difficult for me to choose the most striking feature of the house, the tall pyramid of a roof or the cavernous breezeway that went the length of the house, right down the center, from the broad front porch to the back steps. I'll choose now and say it was that long tunnel of a breezeway. From a position atop the hand-chiseled stone front steps, I recall looking down that tunnel and how the wavering striations in the tongue-and-groove boards of the walls made it appear that the whole thing would have pinched down to nothing if Granddaddy hadn't wisely ended it at the back steps.

The floor plan was simple but ingenious in the way it greatly reduced the number of doors required, which were six in all, and all of them painted black. The six rooms were three bedrooms, a parlor, a dining room, and a kitchen. Each room let out into the dogtrot and, with the exception of a door between the kitchen and dining room, no room connected directly to any other room. Going between any two of the five remaining rooms meant going out into the dogtrot and thence to the other room. Depending on the wind direction, the dogtrot could be an icy wind tunnel in the winter.

What I remember most about my time on Big Branch was the interaction I had with my young uncles, all but one of whom was older than me. They let me and Tommy, an uncle of my own age, play Monopoly with them, and that made me feel pretty good about myself.

We had some board games, a few books and magazines, and like most other mountain homes, Granddaddy's had a big console radio that drew its power from a car battery. All of which is to say that there wasn't much to entertain a houseful of restless young males, so they fought boredom by inventing their own fun. And I was lucky, at age six or seven, to be permitted to tag along when a new adventure was in the offing, but hanging with the big boys could put some wear and tear on one of my size and inexperience.

One summer day we heard one of the two yard dogs baying up in the woods. A couple of the older boys decided that the dog had to be barking at the mouth of a groundhog hole. We might have ignored all the barking, but to routinely do so would teach the dog that it didn't matter what kind of game he was holding at bay, no one was coming to investigate. It wouldn't do to discourage the hunting instinct of the dog, and besides, the younger of the dogs was still in the yard, and he could do with some training.

What kind of training? Why, training in the pursuit and taking of a groundhog. We didn't eat possum, nor to my knowledge did we eat raccoon, but a young groundhog could be stewed or fried and put on the table the same as a rabbit or a squirrel, and if your palate is conditioned to the taste of wild game, groundhog is more than just passable as protein for the table.

We equipped ourselves with a mattock—which is similar to a pickaxe but with a wider flat blade for digging in the earth—and a burlap sack, and we called the young dog to go with us up the hillside. A short climb and we arrived at where the older dog was devoting his full attention to a hole in the ground. The fresh soil that had been flung from the mouth of the burrow was only slightly packed down, and it was smooth and free of vegetation, so it supported the dog's claim that somewhere close below our feet was a groundhog. It was just a matter of blocking up both the main entrance and the back way into the den and digging on a line between the two.

The big boys took turns with the mattock and in a matter of minutes we saw the groundhog. And the main dog saw the groundhog and there was no stopping it before it seized the animal by the back of its neck and began shaking it hard. A dead groundhog wouldn't fit our purpose of training a young dog, so two of the boys held the dog while a third rescued the groundhog from its jaws and stood grasping the animal by its tail.

As the smallest and most useless one of the crew, my job was to squat and hold the mouth of the burlap sack open to receive the groundhog that was squirming and thrashing about. It's fuzzy in my mind; it happened so fast, all I can say is that some things came into dangerous proximity to other things and the groundhog twisted its head around and sank its two big incisors into my shin. It didn't hang on and the presence of bone just under the skin probably prevented a deep wound, so it wasn't as traumatic an event as it may sound. And anyway, we had the groundhog in the bag, we'd all contributed to a successful outcome, and I would be the center of attention when we got home.

Catching a live groundhog was big adventure for a six-year-old, but it was small-time compared to the two biggest events of the year, which had to be the sorghum molasses "stir-off" and the fireworks at Christmas. I was lucky to be staying at Granddaddy Jim's for those festive times.

The "stir-off" took place in the fall when Granddaddy decided his cane patch was ready, when the stalks would give up their sweet juice. The stalks were fed by hand into the sorghum mill, an apparatus with two metal rollers that squeezed the cane and expelled the juice. The mill was mule-powered by old Beck, Granddaddy's big black mule. Hitched to the end of a pole that had once been a tall sapling, old Beck walked in a big circle. The other end of the pole was fastened to the shaft of one roller that had a gear to drive the opposite roller. In that way the juice was captured, and then it was carried in buckets to the big evaporating pan. The pan, about six feet by three feet, and maybe a foot deep, sat over a wood fire that burned late into the night. Granddaddy stirred and skimmed tirelessly, and the syrup thickened, and finally it was poured into big crock containers for keeping.

Neighbors came for what was a social evening and pitched in to help, mainly for the fun of it. The taffy pull was usually the following night when everyone, kids included, gathered at the big dining room table to pull the reheated and thickened molasses into long ropes, then double the ropes, and pull them again, until they cooled to where if you cut pieces with a greased pair of scissors they would harden into what we called "Tough Jack".

The fireworks may have been a one-time event, since it came about when two of my Whitaker uncles returned from their WWII military service with many large boxes of fireworks. They hid them under several of the beds and we kids weren't to learn of them until Christmas Eve. These young men hadn't been part of the big Times Square celebration on VE Day, but that didn't matter; they'd raise hell at the head of Big Branch. When darkness fell that Christmas Eve, every adult, every kid, and some of the neighbors, lit off firecrackers for what seemed like a couple of hours, until the front yard and the ground beyond the fence looked like it had been snowing tiny scraps of paper. Granddaddy put a loud blazing punctuation to it all when he strode to the end of the porch, pointed his Colt .45 automatic pistol toward the crest of a mountain ridge, squeezed off a round, and kept on squeezing the trigger until the magazine was empty and the slide locked in the open position. That was our signal to gather inside and stuff ourselves with sweet treats that was sure to include all the "Tough Jack" our teeth could stand up to.

· · · · · · · ·

I took some gentle kidding from my aunts and uncles. At the big dining table, Aunt Evalee loved to hear me ask for someone to please pass the "burter." And grinning faces turned my way the time I dug into a bowl of boiled turnips thinking they were mashed potatoes. I like stewed turnips now, if they're not overcooked, but I've never again tried mashed turnips.

Grandma Cannie was my mother's step-mother, but she was in every meaningful way my real and true grandmother. A marvelous cook who seemed always to be wearing a white apron and to have her gray hair in a tight bun, Grandma Cannie set out a great variety of tempting dishes, all of it from the garden or the smokehouse, and she did it three times a day. At Christmas, she put into my stocking items identical to those in the stocking of her Tommy; an orange, and various kinds of nuts, none of which were black walnuts or hickory nuts, because both of these varieties fell in abundance from trees on the property. I remember a pair of knee-length brown cotton stockings that she called "golf" socks.

One winter they bought new five-buckle arctics, rubber overshoes, for me and Tommy. We didn't need them when the ground was frozen and the puddles were iced over, so our first opportunity to wear them came after a warm spell had thawed out the muddy puddles along the dirt road between home and school. At the first deep puddle we came to we put our arctics to the test. The mud rose to the second buckle from the top, but nary a drop of cold water made its way in. We congratulated each other and continued on toward the school house, dawdling and jabbering and failing to see that Aunt Peg was catching up with us.

She didn't whip us on the spot—her paddle was on her desk in the school house—so we had time to meditate on our misdeed, and the dread was considerably worse than the paddling we received in front of our classmates. We did wrong and we knew we did wrong; our punishment fit the crime, and justice prevailed, so we harbored no resentment toward our sweet teacher.

Granddaddy assigned me a few chores; everybody had chores. In heating season I carried in coal for the fireplaces that were in every room but the kitchen and dining room. I did it all that winter, and I never made peace with the dented five-gallon tin bucket that contrived to be empty every time I looked at it. The coal shed sat a mere one hundred feet from the front steps, out by the little branch that flowed nearby, but the tall paling fence required that I first walk away from the coal shed and out through the front gate, and then double back to the shed.

I could have carried lighter loads and made more trips, but I opted to fill the bucket to the top and heft it with both hands as I puffed and grunted and made frequent stops along the way. Hard work for a six-year-old, but here's the thing; it didn't kill me. It was just one of many experiences that I think inured me to hard work and conditioned me to do a job without complaining. I didn't love hauling in coal back then, but I believe that I reaped long-term benefits from not having been coddled.

· · · · · · · ·

The coal came from Granddaddy's "coal bank", which was the sort of small coal mine that the more ambitious households maintained for their own consumption. Black powder obviated the labor and tedium of going at the face of the coal with a pick. Granddaddy, in his khaki twill shirt and trousers and sweat-stained suspenders, leaned on the breast plate of a long iron hand-auger and cranked it to bore a deep hole into the wall of coal. Next he rolled some pages of old newspaper into a tube and filled it with black powder, which he then inserted into the hole. He then inserted the fuse, one that was sufficiently long to allow him time to get outside ere it burnt to where it ignited the powder. As he touched a sulfur match to the tip of the fuse he'd yell, "Fire in the hole," and head quickly for daylight.

Once he was safely clear and standing with us, his helpers, to the side of the dark hole in the mountainside, Granddaddy would remove his old felt hat and glasses and mop his brow with a red bandanna. "Any second, now," he'd say, and just about then would come the resounding boom, echoing off the far mountainside as chunks of coal came flying past us and went tumbling and rattling through the brush down the hillside. Some waste was inevitable, but a goodly pile of coal would lie on the floor of the mine waiting to be shoveled into a sled and hauled down the hill behind Old Beck, Granddaddy's big black mule.

If any mountain family was ever more nearly self-sufficient and lived any better off what nature made available in exchange for wise preparation and hard work, I've yet to hear of it, and I'm confident I never shall.

I think my granddaddy always spoke his mind and offered his opinion when asked, and that he never conceded a disputed notion unless faced with a convincing argument to the contrary. He was a proud man who had made a decent home for his large family, and I doubt that any other man in Letcher County could have worked his land to better results than Granddaddy did. He was a religious man and as confident in the rightness of his religion as he was in the way he operated his farm. When he spoke he spoke with conviction, but "dad blame" was as close as he'd come to cussing. On one occasion I saw what a limiting and burdensome thing it was for my granddaddy to vent his anger and loathing through the muffling gag of a Primitive Baptist lexicon of "choice words".

It must have been in the evening, after chores and before supper, for several of us were gathered on the front porch when the conversation grew loud and I tuned in to what the adults were saying.

Two of Granddaddy's sons had seen military service in Europe during the recently-ended war, so Granddaddy had opinions about various wartime leaders. The topic this time was general George S. Patton, and Granddaddy laid into "Old Blood and Guts" Patton for his having slapped two GIs who had been diagnosed as suffering from "Battle Fatigue". Patton had branded them as cowards, for which Granddaddy deemed Patton to be worse than a coward, and who knows but what Granddaddy would have employed "sonofabitch", or even "goddamn sonofabitch", but for the fact of his tongue being effectively bridled against such useful and universally understood vituperation. I don't remember what adjectives Granddaddy used, but, having learned my own cuss words in Roxana, I'm sure that "sinner" or "abomination" wouldn't have moved me to shout, "You tell 'em, Granddaddy."

· · · · · · · ·

I liked being at Granddaddy's, with all the young aunts and uncles paying me a little attention from time to time. But I didn't mind leaving the head of Big Branch when, with no forewarning, my mother came to take me back to Roxana, where she managed somehow to gather her children all under the same roof. There we remained but a short time, and then we split up once again and went in several different directions.

·

While living with the Calihans on Pace's Branch Jim
and I would spend an occasional weekend with Uncle
Isaac and aunt Gladys and our cousins on Kings
Creek. Their home at the time was the same house
where Stephen and Larcena Hogg had raised their
large family. Here Jim sits in the front, me in back,
both of us astride Maude, Cousin Wade's gentle pony.

Sam: A good mule was essential to life at the head of Pace's Branch.

9 Pace's Branch

In the spring of 1946 I was just beginning to collect some memories that might last, and that was when Mother had her plan worked out for how to temporarily stash her children and get a new hold on life. She was bound for Lexington, Kentucky, and I, along with older brother Jim, was bound for the home of Bill and Mary Calihan at the head of Pace's Branch.

I didn't know then that Mother's term as postmistress had come to an end and that she was unemployed and broke and at the end of her rope as the family provider. I was dumb as a sheep about why we were leaving Roxana and about where we were headed. I wasn't consulted on such matters, and if my mother even hinted at why she was going to Lexington, I don't remember the conversation. I learned only that she had worked it out with the Calihans for Jim and me to stay with them for some indefinite period.

With such a large extended family as ours was, though, one might ask why my mother didn't just board my brother and me with relatives. I can guess at why Mother didn't want her children boarding any longer with relatives—she was afraid of losing us. If a child welfare agency were to come prying, they might say that if we were being cared for by an aunt or a grandfather, then, okay, these children don't need to be moved, and never mind, Mrs. Hogg, about your plans to provide for them on your own; you're in no position to do so.

In that, the child welfare people would have been more right than they might have suspected. Mother had only the slightest experience in working for wages, with the small exception being when for a brief period she served as the Roxana postmistress. Her appointment had come by way of local friends with influence who saw her plight and sought to help out.

It wasn't a job she was well suited for, however, so it didn't last long. She must then have seen Lexington as the best place for an inexperienced person to find an entry-level job and gain some work experience and then try for something better.

I was uninformed about the whys of it all, but I remember well the day that Jim and I left Roxana to go live with the Calihans. They sent Delbert H.—about age fourteen and soon to leave their care—to escort me and Jim to their house at the head of Pace's Branch. I looked over my shoulder at the home I was leaving and at my mother, waving goodbye, until my view was blocked by the dusty sycamore trees that stood along the river bank. As we walked along the gravel road up Kings Creek I was seeing everything as if for the first time, and I don't know why, but I wasn't crying or feeling anything other than the newness of it all.

We walked roughly one mile along the county-maintained gravel road to the mouth of Pace's Branch, and another long mile along a footpath to the last house, at the head of the hollow.

The few homes near the mouth of the hollow were within sight of each other, and they showed some care in their upkeep. Then came a stretch of a half mile along which were only deep woods on either side of the meandering shady path.

The hollow opened up considerably as we neared its upper end, and we passed two more homes before we came in sight of Bill and Mary's place. First was the home of Clovis Calihan. I came to learn that Clovis was a part-time farmer, whose main job was that of "section hand", meaning that he helped maintain a "section" of the L & N Railroad track. He arose each workday before daylight to don his coveralls and work boots and hike out of the hollow with his "dinner bucket" in his hand. Like so many miners who lived up the hollows, his workday, when you add the long walk to and from his work site, ran from pre-dawn to early darkness.

Still, section hand seemed to me to be the best sort of job one could have. I'd seen the men arrive at Roxana and board a "motor car", which wasn't, as one might think, an automobile, for how could an automobile travel on the railroad track? No, a "motor car" was a boxy little motorized conveyance on four steel wheels and with side-facing bench seats that accommodated a half-dozen riders. It scooted along the rails to take a crew to the work site for that particular day. I didn't know of policemen and firemen; my dream was to ride upon a railroad motor car.

A quarter mile farther up Pace's Branch we came upon a house that looked solid and handsome, and rather too fine for Pace's Branch. Instead of the familiar, cheap-to-build, board-and-batten structure with a gable roof, this fine dwelling featured a hip roof covered in tin, and pale yellow weatherboard siding, all trimmed in white, including columns on a front porch that ran the width of the house. Here lived Bill's brother, Lloyd Calihan, his wife, Nora, and two or three school-age children. Lloyd's hillside farm was still his livelihood, one that wasn't supplemented by a job in a coal mine or on the railroad. Owner's pride showed in the orderly appearance of his outbuildings, none of which perched on the steep hillside behind the main house, but were set in a line along his side of the hollow. We walked past his barn, and when we came to cross a rail fence at the edge of his property, we saw in the distance the home of Bill and Mary Calihan.

This Calihan house, unlike the downstream houses that faced the footpath and the little stream, sat facing the long view down the hollow. A board-and-batten structure of rough-sawn lumber, it was a faded sky blue with vivid orange trim. But that was just the front; the remaining three sides were bare boards weathered to a silvery gray. The house sat a few feet higher up than the path by which we approached, such that I saw the floor joists all the way back to the rearmost of the tree-stump pilings that kept it off the ground and maintained a surprisingly level floor inside.

Certainly it looked better to me than our first Roxana house, the shotgun shack that featured rotted planks in the front porch and was clad in scarred and scabbed red imitation-brick siding, and that straddled a drainage ditch.

Old Watch, the Calihan's big black and white dog, ambled out from his dusty wallow beneath the high porch to be the first to greet the three of us. As we stepped onto the porch, Bill rocked his ladder-back chair down onto four legs and rose heavily to his feet. "Howdy, boys," he said, "how're things in Roxanie?" Roxanie, not Roxana. Roxana is a pretty name, but maybe to some minds it was just too pretty for our dusty little crossroads hamlet.

But Bill's pronunciation had naught to do with pride or shame; I think it was just the way mountaineers said words that outsiders would have ended with the short "a" sound, *ah*. I'm reasonably sure it was because they didn't want to come across as sounding high-bred, fancy, or citified. I knew a man named Ira, and his daddy always called him "Arrie". Literacy was a little spotty in the "hollers". Most could read and write, but proper spelling on paper didn't carry over to their speech. Elizabethan English colored the speech of those who learned their words solely by ear, and I feel privileged to have experienced the mountain vernacular before I was rehabilitated in the school system of Fayette County, Kentucky.

Some words pertaining to human reproduction, for instance, held different meanings for us than they did for outsiders. *Cuckold* was such a word, and old Bill, once he got to know us—or perhaps it was his way of *getting* to know us—liked to repeat a little joke that shows how *cuckold* served as a verb in the place of *fornicate*, which was a word you'd never hear except from the mouth of a fire-breathing preacher.

The setup: Teacher desired that little Johnny spell and give the definition for the word *crow*, and she saw right away that little Johnny was stumped for an answer.

Teacher: Johnny, what does a rooster do first thing each morning?

Johnny: Our old rooster cuckolds a hen.

Teacher: (suppressing a snigger) Okay, but then what does your rooster do?

Johnny: He hops another'n an' cuckolds hit, too.

Bill was a portly old fellow in overalls, the bib of which was stained with tobacco spit that had fallen short of the end of the porch. His plug hat had holes in it and he was in some need of a haircut. To picture his wife, Mary, think of Granny Clampett of television's long-running *Beverly Hillbillies*. Mary, in her long full skirt and ever-present apron, wore high-topped men's work shoes and kept her gray hair in a tight bun.

Jim and I each carried our wardrobe of extra overalls, T-shirts, and socks in a single paper bag, and settling in with the Calihans was easy and quickly done. We were surprised to see them preparing to go to bed at the early edge of darkness, but they pointed us to a featherbed and blew out the lamp, and that was that. With not even a radio and no light to read by, that first night was a long one.

I don't remember remarking on the absence of electricity. After all, the only things that had used electric current in our Roxana home were the bare bulbs hanging in a couple of rooms, and the remaining rooms were still lighted by kerosene lamps. Neither did we remark on the absence of indoor plumbing, as before bedtime Jim and I looked for the outdoor privy. And we looked. And we looked. And looked some more. Ohh-kay, where's that little house out behind the big house? Where's that Little Brown Shack, that fixture that no backyard was without, that humble hut that Billy Edd Wheeler was to pay sentimental homage to in his 1965 hit song *Ode to the Little Brown Shack out Back*? Wherever it was or wasn't, we brushed aside the missing convenience with not much comment, and then we did what comes naturally. Out behind the barn, naturally.

Jim and I disdained to ask about the missing outhouse. Our supplemental parents didn't bring it up; Jim was too bashful to ask, and as I'd never believed a smelly privy to be strictly necessary, I didn't much care. For a couple of weeks we tried out a new place each day. And it was perhaps months before we detected any evidence of bodily function south of Bill's belly, and for all we were ever to learn of Mary's habits, she was an angel who flew under cover of darkness into the woods to a moss-lined bower of bowel release.

We couldn't stay fastened to the question and the search. Why be curious about one matter in particular when everything else seemed so passing strange? We accepted it as natural and therefore not something to trouble our minds with. If something could so easily be done without, then why tax oneself to build and maintain it? If you could not send away the unwanted product of your grunting efforts, as surely we could not, not without a flush toilet, then why would we want to save it all in one place? We were, after all, the last house on the branch. The rare visitor that came to the front porch had no need to go past the house, and past the house were some two hundred acres of privacy. I came later to recognize it for the sanitarily superior system it was as compared to a too-close outhouse.

Did the Calihans squat upon chamber pots? I saw no sign that they did, and we, all four of us, slept in the same room. Bill slept in his bed, and Mary slept in hers, while Jim and I shared a soft featherbed in a corner. Bill would step out of his stiff overalls to reveal the long drawers that Mary had made for him. She made them from a fabric she called "factory", a type of unprinted calico made from unbleached and often not-fully-processed cotton. His drawers showed dark specks that were bits of cotton seed husks. Mary didn't make any drawers for me and Jim, and I'm hard pressed now to recall wearing underwear of any kind at all. We didn't wear long johns in the summer time, and I don't remember any briefs or boxers. But we wouldn't have been naked under our overalls, wouldn't have stripped bare at bedtime, not in the same sleeping room with Bill and Mary who were so guarded with their bodies. But as to the important matter of bowel regularity, I never once saw a chamber pot of any kind, so I must conclude that their practice was as uncomplicated as it was for the earliest settlers.

Be all that as it may, and it may be that I have simply forgotten some parts of my experience at the head of Pace's Branch, but even if in this instance I have remembered correctly, it is no reflection on anyone. And here is why I say that. It was a different time and place, far different perhaps than I am capable of conveying to urban dwellers who are conditioned to conventions that are essential for people living side by side. The Calihans didn't live next to anyone, and the foxes, raccoons, and red-tailed hawks couldn't have cared less; neither they nor the Calihans knew anything of homeowner's associations with rules and restrictions. Bill and Mary wisely devoted their labors to tasks that had undeniable utilitarian purpose. Luxury to them was food to last through a long winter and coal to throw on the stone fireplace. And that's no different than it was for many a pioneering family whose own experience in settling the American West was concurrent with the early lives of Bill and Mary Calihan.

This has been a long way of saying that you had to be there, but since you weren't there, I hope you'll take my word for it.

· · · · · · · ·

I need to pause here and rethink what I said about the absence of "indoor plumbing". I don't know why I even mentioned it, since Jim nor I could possibly have been surprised to learn that the Calihan place had no plumbing. We'd never seen plumbing and wouldn't have recognized it if we'd stubbed a toe on a galvanized iron pipe.

The only thing I ever saw there that had the capacity to conduct fluid was some shiny copper tubing of about one-half inch to one inch in diameter. It was shaped into a coil that was about two feet long and twelve inches in diameter. I'd see it from time to time on the top shelf of a closet in Mary's quilting room, and then it would go missing for a spell. We weren't to learn why that strange tubing kept leaving and returning to that closet shelf until many years after we'd left pace's Branch. The revelation came when one of our uncles told Jim, and Jim later told me, why it was that he and two of his brothers had come once on foot all the way to the head of Pace's Branch and pretended to us that it was strictly to pay a visit to their two young nephews.

As our uncle explained it to Jim, the real reason for them dropping by the Calihan house from time to time was for the purpose of purchasing moonshine whiskey, good moonshine whiskey, something they could drink without fear of going blind or being afflicted with "Jake Leg"[4] and having to walk funny for the rest of their lives.

So, the coil of copper tubing that I glimpsed from time to time had to have been the condensing coil, the "worm", for the Calihan's moonshine still. The precise location of their moonshine operation remains a mystery to me. Jim thinks that the cooker for heating the mash was small enough to sit on top of the small kitchen stove and that when not in use it was stowed in the attic above the kitchen. This fact would explain another mystery of long standing, and that is the question of why Bill sometimes loaded a long "mill sack" of shelled corn across Sam's withers and rode to the mill to have it ground. It wasn't for making cornbread, as the cornmeal for that was store-bought and brought home in a paper sack with a brand name on it. And if it wasn't for making cornbread, that leaves only one reason why the Calihan's needed so much more of the stuff. Cornmeal is a basic ingredient in the mash from which moonshine whiskey is distilled. Why tip off the grocer by buying more cornmeal than one household could possibly use up in cornbread when you had shelled corn on hand by the bushel? If Bill had confided in Jim and me, and if he'd shared some of his moonshine money, I bet we'd have worked harder at making a good corn crop.

---

[4]**Jake Leg:** In the Prohibition Era, an estimated 30,000-50,000 persons developed partial paralysis of the legs from drinking moonshine to which had been added a patent medicine called **Jamaica Ginger** (or, "Jake"), which itself had been altered by the addition of Tricresyl phosphate (TCP) in a effort to fool Treasury Department testers as to its legally-required content of solids.

That day of our arrival, April 22, 1946, was my birthday, and somewhere on our way to meet the Calihans for the first time, Delbert, our escort, learned of the fact and laid me face-down on the hillside just off our path and gave me seven licks for my attained age, plus one good hard one "to grow on".

Delbert would soon leave the Calihans to go work in a coal mine, but not so soon as to keep me and Jim from discovering his Lucky Strikes and finding out how much better factory cigarettes tasted than did those consisting of rabbit tobacco[5] rolled in newspaper. We stole the tobacco from Delbert, but I expect he'd have shared if we'd asked. One thing that he shared freely, and with some bravado, was his newfound knowledge of how to set off a stick of dynamite—in a manner that placed expediency ahead of overwrought notions about safety. I'm sure that if there'd been any dynamite around the Calihan place fourteen-year-old Delbert would have given a live demonstration. As it was, though, he acted out how he would have crimped a blasting cap on the end of a fuse by biting it together with his teeth, how he'd have used a nail to punch a hole in the side of the dynamite stick and inserted the cap, and then how he would have put a match to the loose end of the fuse, hollered "fire in the hole", and ran like hell.

I'm sure that Bill and Mary must have said whatever they felt we needed to hear in order to feel welcome and wanted. But their head-of-the-holler parlance took some getting used to. "Scace" for scarce. And as I mentioned earlier, their conjugation of the verb "help" was a revelation. The past tense was "holp". He tried, but it just couldn't be holp.

Bill was literate, in that he could read, as he did everyday on the front porch as he leaned against the wall in a ladder-back chair and studied his small New Testament or the Cincinnati Post newspaper that was two days old and secondhand from his brother Lloyd just down the branch. But he never preached to me and Jim. He did, however, regale us from time to time with salacious stories and ribald rhymes. I believe he did it out of his affection for two little boys and a desire to bond with us in a way that would give him leave to be himself.

---

[5] **Rabbit tobacco** is one of many names given to *Gnaphalium obtusifolium*, a member of the aster family of wild flowering plants. At its base is the cluster of crinkly leaves that rural southern boys have since days of yore rolled into cigarettes and smoked as a rite of passage.

We did have to work, milking two Holstein cows, Ruby and Spot, and feeding them and feeding Sam, the Calihan's ancient mule, plus planting and hoeing corn, and harvesting the bloody same. On the other hand, we had freedom, that blessed freedom that's never to be known by most of today's over-governed children. We were free of excessive parental concern as to how we might injure ourselves; there were simply too many hazards to go focusing on one in particular.

Bill and Mary, I'm sure, didn't wish us maimed or killed, but they were past the age where they wanted to climb the steep slopes and see what the hell we were up to up in the woods. But Bill spied on us with an old pair of binoculars, and that turned out on one occasion to be fortuitous, however much it terminated some great fun.

A city dweller might think of wild grape vines as the tender tendrils in an abandoned vineyard, but in the hills of eastern Kentucky a grapevine is a hardy creeper, often as thick and strong as the bowline on an ocean liner. A Pace's Branch grapevine grows until its uppermost appendages are fully entwined with the top branches of a tall tree. And if that tree is situated on sloping ground, and if a barefoot mountain boy sees in it the potential for a free thrill ride, then you can bet that grapevine will be severed from its roots and used for a swing.

Jim and I weren't willfully reckless; we were just uninformed about the many ways of maiming or killing ourselves that were all so close at hand. We found a perfect specimen of a thrill-ride vine. We took a double-bit axe up the hill and chopped the big vine in two just below where it ran horizontally for a few inches to make a fine notch to accommodate our butts when we swung out on it. The tree was tall and the ground sloped steeply away from it, down to a boulder-strewn gully that in a downpour was a roaring cataract. You could have hoisted a piano with that stout vine, so where was the danger?

A dull axe and an iron-hard vine made the chopping a slow, sweaty job. But with adventure in the offing we were undeterred, because we saw what would have been obvious to anyone—this would be the perfect swingin' vine.

Being of sufficient length and unobstructed by low limbs, the vine would swing through a long shallow arc. We never dwelt overly on the possibility that it might not return us to solid ground, that it might leave one of us suspended mid-swing at a height from which a fall could only end in our shattered and bloody remains upon the boulders below. If the thought did occur to us, it must have goaded us to push off with a long run 'n go.

With calloused bare feet slapping against the shale outcropping, we'd push off and swing across the yawning chasm, screaming all the way and praying that our push-off was enough to propel us back to safety. I suppose if you're truly ignorant of the risks, you're not as apt to tense up and make a fatal misstep, but if either of us had lost our grip at a hundred feet above the rocks the only soft landing we could count on would involve a child-sized pine coffin covered in gray velvet.

Rattlesnakes. No one had said a word to me about the damn rattlesnakes. I was serenely ignorant and took no precautions against being bitten by a rattlesnake. Soon after our arrival in April, the Calihans began preparing for planting time, and I got to see what it was to plow a hillside corn patch. Earl H., Delbert's older brother who was recently returned from army service in England, manned the plow behind Sam, the steady old mule.

With nothing else to occupy me I wandered among the piles of rocks that had been there from when the land had first been cleared and made tillable. It was near one of these piles that I saw my first rattlesnake. It was a baby rattler, and in that I took ignorant comfort, ignorant because as I was to learn, a snake so small would have been recently born, complete with a potent starter shot of venom, and not hatched from an egg either, but directly from inside its live mother. And how likely was it that the mother was somewhere within the rock pile? My ignorance may have saved me, for I just stood gazing at the cute baby snake and made no commotion that might have disturbed the mama snake.

I have mentioned how Bill would often sit at the far end of the porch reading a tiny *New Testament*, one of the palm-sized booklets such as the mountain missionaries gave away when they visited our Kings Creek schools to indoctrinate "unchurched" children in the tenets of the Christian Faith. I recall the times when the same two ladies would come to our school and set up their easel and illustrate their Bible stories with felt cutouts of Jesus, as a white lamb, and other figures that must have been His disciples. They'd leave us with the promise that if any of us memorized five Bible verses they'd reward us with a small booklet containing the Gospels of Matthew, Mark, Luke, and John. I met the test and was proud to receive my little booklet. For a third-grader it was pretty dry reading, so I don't think I got very far into the Gospels.

On reflection I'm glad I didn't look too closely at that little booklet, because it wasn't long afterward that my youthful ignorance of the Gospels allowed me to collect one of those memories of a malapropism so resplendently funny and so chastening as to guarantee that if I would but remember how it felt I'd never again take myself too seriously. Allow me to jump ahead about three years in my story, to a time in Lexington, Kentucky when a neighbor boy and school mate invited me to attend his Sunday school.

I forgot the lesson almost as soon as it was over, but I won't ever forget the closing song, which to my ears and to my religiously-untutored mind was about some fellow named Matthew "Marcluking" John. I'd never before heard that odd-sounding adjective, *marcluking*. It was so silly that I had to wonder how I'd let myself be tricked into attending. The memory, so firmly etched by my sense of having been duped, was of course a time bomb waiting to go off and set me on my presumptuous ass when I should inevitably learn just a little more about the four men who wrote—or as some scholars say, did not write—the Gospels that are named for them.

I might well have forgotten all about old "Marclukin' John" if not for a blurb I saw in *Reader's Digest* some twenty years later, a tale that affirmed for me that while words make pictures, it takes a wicked sense of humor in combination with innocent open-mindedness to see the wonderfully absurd versions of said pictures. As did the child who sat in his family's church pew, torn between pity and an attack of spit-spewing giggles, as they sang a hymn whose main refrain sounded like "Gladly, the Cross-Eyed Bear".

For his part, though, Bill Calihan never sermonized to me and Jim, except on infrequent occasions when he drew from scripture to emphasize a point.

The Calihans never left the head of the hollow to attend any church services. Since most church services were some miles away, attending would have meant a tiring trip and time away from the never-ending farm chores. But I believe they were just so busy scratching out a living in an unforgiving place that they had little time for religion, politics, or world affairs, none of which ever bore much on events along Pace's Branch.

I believe, and I am grateful to think, that my time there was entirely free of any sort of indoctrination. Certainly, I heard some questionable opinions related as fact, but they lay lightly upon my brain, were carried for a while, and then discarded without harsh judgment of their source. In the main, excepting a few ghost stories, I wasn't brainwashed to believe anything other than what was plain and demonstrable fact.

Later, during my childhood in Lexington, Kentucky, I was still as susceptible as any other eleven-year-old might be to the fervent blandishments of a Baptist preacher who, out of his sincere belief in what he was ordained to do, seduced me into answering the "altar call". I recall walking down the aisle, tears glistening on my cheeks, and questioning how others of the congregation could remain seated and unmoved by the preacher's rapturous plea that we save our sorry souls, today, in the waning days before the "End Times".

That was the beginning of a forty-year period of intermittent spiritual angst during which I continued semi-regular church attendance, first as a Baptist and later, after I met my wife-to-be, as a Lutheran.

I may be fooling myself to think it's even possible , but if I were asked today I'd say that I like to think for myself. My time with the Calihans was three years of freedom from the influence of any inflexible doctrines except for what was taught in the Letcher County school system. Nobody was telling me that I was going to Hell just because I couldn't recite from memory any parts of their particular brand of religious dogma. I like to think that in me was planted a germ of belief in my own capacity for rational thought, and that it blossomed in later life when I came to think, for instance, that if I'd been born in India I might well be fluent in the tenets of Hinduism and know little, if anything at all, about the Judeo-Christian Tradition. I seemed to me then, as it does now, that what one is schooled to believe depends quite a lot on where one happens to have been born.

• • • • • • • •

The Calihan house offered little in the way of entertainment for a child, but Bill and Mary must have nonetheless understood that young boys need outlets for their energy and inquisitiveness. I recall one Friday evening in particular when Bill saw that we were bored silly and said, "Alright, why don't you two just go on down to Junior's and radio with 'em?" Junior was Bill's nephew and was at the time living in and caring for the house that belonged to his daddy Lloyd, Bill's brother. Junior had a radio. No electricity, but still he had a radio.

The radio was playing when we got to Junior's and we heard a fiddle and a banjo and the raucous laughter from one of the several live "Barn Dance" shows that were in those days broadcast by 50,000-Watt stations whose signals reached throughout the southeastern US. We enjoyed sitting with Junior and his young wife and listening and laughing at what we heard. They were young and uncomplicated, and it wasn't awkward at all for me and Jim to be their guests for the evening. Junior gave us a can of Pabst Blue Ribbon beer to share and later said, "How 'bout we all go possum huntin'?"

It was my first ever taste of beer, and I liked it. I don't remember if half a beer buzzed my eight-year-old head. Probably not much, for I recall well that we'd scarcely started our ascent of the moonlit hillside when Junior's hound sounded his bark that announced, "I got a possum up a tree here, so y'all come on right now."

High in the top limbs of a Poplar tree the possum's eyes reflected back at us the light cast by Junior's shiny brass carbide lamp[6]. Junior nodded at my brother and said, "Go shake him out for us, Jimbo," so Jim was the hero this time around as he eagerly shinnied up the tree. He arrived at the limb on whose far end sat the possum with his lips drawn away from his little white needle teeth, hissing ferociously.

I don't recall whether or not Jim succeeded in shaking the possum off the limb, but I hope he didn't, because the dog would have fastened its jaws on the possum's neck and killed it in an instant, and I'd already seen a few animals being maltreated by drunken yahoos back in Roxana.

I think that Junior just had us out for the hunt to hear his hound bay when he struck the scent and then to hear his very different bark when he had his quarry up a tree. Whatever the case, it was high adventure for me and Jim. We'd listened to our favorite kind of radio program, broad country humor and hillbilly music; we'd had our first PBR; and we'd gone hunting, also a first for us. It was a memorable evening.

Pace's branch was entirely without electricity, and I still wonder how Junior managed to recharge the big 6-volt car battery that powered his radio. I can only suppose that when the battery was drained he sacked it up and saddled his big mealy-nosed red mule for a

---

[6] **Carbide lamps** are simple lamps that produce and burn acetylene (C_2H_2) which is created by the reaction of calcium carbide (CaC_2) with water.

ride into Roxana and a visit to Hiram Mitchell's store, where there was electricity.

A lot of trouble, one might say today, but it wasn't as though Junior or anybody else up Pace's Branch kept to a Soccer Mom schedule. That kind of insanity was fifty years in the future, and let's just don't get me started on that. I'll just say how thankful I am that my brother and I had unstructured playtime that was virtually unlimited and a world of self-directed adventure that few children of today will ever experience. I hasten to say that I don't hold Soccer Moms—bless 'em for the job they do so devotedly—to blame for their children's lamentable lack of free time. The fact of it just saddens me, that's all.

Christmas at the Calihan's was noted but not much observed beyond Bill's little joke of being the first to yell, "Christmas gift!" which meant that he'd pulled one over on me or Jim and now we were on the hook; we owed him a present, but we weren't meant to ever make good on it. That was it; no stockings were hung by the sooty chimney, and no one went to the barnyard on Christmas Eve to see if the animals talked.

Our mother didn't fail me and Jim, though. A week or so before our first Christmas on Pace's Branch, we learned that two packages awaited us at the Roxana post office. We were permitted to make the Roxana trip by ourselves, and there we found the packages waiting for us. Of course we ripped the wrappings off as soon as we were across the bridge and had turned on the road back toward Pace's Branch. In one package was a Monopoly set, in the other, a toy truck. We couldn't do anything with the Monopoly set as we walked along, but since the tin truck had a pull string, we dragged it the two miles back to the Calihan's.

It almost seems that I can recall every stone that little truck bumped over. The tin truck had two tiny headlights, but we spent the life of the two D-cell batteries in those two miles, wasted them in the bright daylight, and since batteries didn't grow on Pace's Branch trees, we never got to see if the headlights made it more fun to drag the truck around in the dark.

The Monopoly set was a godsend though, and in Mary's quilting room we played Monopoly endlessly. It was the spare room in the three-room house, unheated and used only in warm weather when Mary did her quilting. She would let her quilting frame down from the ceiling, gather the pieces she'd cut from cast-off clothing and linens, and sew them into her quilt pattern, which was usually "wedding rings" or "stars".

Jim and I didn't mind the chill in that room. We lay on the bare floor in our winter coats, each hoarding the rent money we collected and plotting the other's financial ruin. "I think I'll just rest here in jail while you go bust. You just land on Park Place or Boardwalk, my friend, and I'll have your crappy little Oriental Avenue." But I don't think "crappy" was in our cuss-word lexicon at the time; we probably said "*sorry ass* little Oriental Avenue." *Sorry* was sometimes used in the context of ruefulness, but I most often heard it said of some person or other, usually a man, that he was *sorry*, meaning that he drank too much, couldn't hold a job, or he let his "chillern run aroun' in rags."

At the Calihans were some few books, one or two thick mail-order catalogs, some fairly recent copies of the *Cincinnati Post* newspaper, and one old almanac. I tried to read some of each one and ended up rereading a few. The almanac had on its cover the "Zodiac Man" with a flap of skin peeled away from his abdomen to reveal his entrails. I was intrigued, but I didn't learn much about planting "by the signs". Once Bill caught me and Jim in the quilting room with a catalog and saw that it was opened to women's intimate apparel. I don't recall whether or not he was grinning when he asked if we were studying "twitchets". It was a new word for us, but in the setting, and considering who was doing the asking, our prurient little minds were quick to grasp its anatomical nature.

I pored eagerly over the comics section in the *Cincinnati Post*. Starved as I was for reading material, the characters in the "funny papers" etched themselves in my brain. *Curly Kayo*, affable boxer; *Joe Palooka*, who was much the same; *Mutt and Jeff*, the long and the short of comic blunderers; *Nancy*, so recently dismissed by bloggers for being mainly unfunny; *Alley Oop*, caveman; the single-panel cartoons, *Out our Way* and *Our Boarding House*, the latter featuring fez-wearing, cigar-smoking Major Amos B. Hoople (Egad, Madam! Puff, Puff. Hak-Kaff!).

I found two or three comic books, in one of which were images that for their staying power might have been impressed upon my brain only yesterday. This was 1946-1947 and very soon after a time when comic book heroes had gone to war against the Axis Powers. Frankenstein's Monster was rampaging across a European battlefield and venting his extreme pique by smiting German soldiers, and officers in particular, left and right, something like Samson destroying the Philistines. Frankie's appearance terrorized the jack-booted Nazis, and then, one by one, as they cowered with mouths agape and one eye magnified by that hated Nazi symbol, the monocle, he bludgeoned them to death with whatever blunt instrument was closest to hand.

I discovered four or five titles from the *Big Little* Books that were nearing the end of their popularity by then. These heavily-illustrated little books were about the size of a four-inch length of 2 x 4 lumber. My little trove included *Dick Tracy*, the square-jawed crime fighter always on the chase after disfigured villains, including Prune face, Flathead Jones, and the Mole; *Li'l Abner* and the folks of Dogpatch, USA; *Red Ryder* and his cowboy adventures with his young Indian sidekick, Little Beaver; *Roy Rogers* in *Robbers' Roost*. Coming to the end of the last of these marvelous little books left me yearning for more.

These great little books sold for fifteen cents in their heyday; now they bring $29.99 on eBay and other websites. They were free to me of course, but I'd have had my money's worth if I'd paid ten bucks apiece in 1947 dollars. They were that stimulating to my imagination. No other written materials, and especially not the pap in school readers, can share credit for igniting that eager little flame that grew into my love for the books that have kept the faith and allowed me to live an inner life unconstrained by time or place.

If we'd had cable TV, video games, and the Internet in the 1940s and 50s, would I have seen and remembered as much of my real world as I now so easily recall? Not likely, as I was the type of child who'd have grown pale from Vitamin D deficiency that would have been owing to all the time spent indoors hunched over a keyboard and staring at a monitor until my eyeballs bled.

I was a child on Pace's Branch, and it would be another ten years before I'd read John Steinbeck's *Grapes of Wrath*, but even then I wasn't ready yet to reflect on the rich milieu of characters I'd been among in the flesh. That insight came only haltingly. After panning that stream for six decades, though, if I relax my mind and drift back, I find I'm still apt to stumble upon some nuggets.

I had a mother, but as I had no daddy, to the people of Pace's Branch that made me an orphan. I learned this from an "orphan" who lived with his mother and several bachelor uncles in a place near the mouth of the branch. Soon after we first met him, Sherman D. was all sympathy and commiseration, sharing with me and Jim that he, too, was an orphan. Sherman may have been my age, but then his scrawny form might have been misleading; he smoked Camel cigarettes and often had a cud of Beechnut chewing tobacco bulging one side of his thin face.

For all his elfin size and overt friendliness, little Sherman smelled of threat. As he gave us his welcoming ramble, citing the dubious sameness of our respective family circumstances, he fiddled with a sizable folding knife and did little to hide his notion of himself as a bad boy. But he wouldn't do anything mean to two fellow orphans.

To seal his promise, Sherman gifted me and Jim with two oddly-shaped balloons. They were long and whitish, but I could see clear through them. Unlike any balloons I'd ever seen, they had long nipples at their ends. "They ain't real balloons," he said with an air of confidentiality, "they just some old rubbers." At the time I didn't ponder what he meant by *old*.

From what I came to learn about Sherman's domestic situation, I can surmise now that his curious behavior didn't stem so much from poor parenting—he wasn't neglected or willfully abused—as it did from being cosseted by rough-edged bachelor uncles who still lived in the same household. I'm sure I must have envied Sherman.

• • • • • • • •

The head of Pace's Branch was a sheltering place for two little boys. Bill and Mary Calihan, by their sweat and by their wits, had made for themselves a life that, however plain it was, fully satisfied their needs and wants, and they shared all they had with my brother and me. Some lessons were hard, and it's taken time for me to appreciate them, but the learning has lasted, and I look back with gratitude.

Walking into an ambush on the way home from school.

10   The Three Rs and a W

Three Rs, for readin', ritin', an' rith'matic. And a W, for the whippings I got. That sums up the second of my two forays through the fourth grade at Lower Kings Creek School. I had two runs at the fourth grade, but getting set back a year wasn't because of anything I did or didn't do; it was because of what happened to Mary Calihan. One snowy day as she was heading out to the barn to do the milking, Mary lost her footing and pitched down the hill and into the side of the house and cracked a bone in her arm. With our cook/farmhand/laundry maid laid up, someone else had to cook, clean, do laundry, feed the poultry and livestock, milk the cows, and on and on, attending to an endless list of daily chores. There was nothing for it but for Jim and me to stay home and miss several weeks of school as we covered for her. Before the next school year began, our Aunt Gladys, as legal guardian, agreed with school officials that I required a do-over of the fourth grade and Jim would likewise benefit by repeating the fifth grade.

This disruption, when added to the fact of my living in a strange place without my mother, may account for the trouble I made for myself that second time around.

I knew better than to act out for my foster parents, the Calihans, who brooked no nonsense, so I rebelled at school. I took lickings from my teacher. I knew I deserved them, and I didn't resent them too much, and they didn't poison my memories of that time, a time that I know now was the ending of an era, the era of the rural two-room school house.

In the hills and hollows of Letcher County it was more feasible to place a clapboard two-room school house every couple of miles than it was to purchase, operate, and maintain a fleet of school buses just to haul the children in grades K-8 to fewer but larger schools. We had no lunchroom and therefore no cooks, we were our own janitors, and there were no health care persons or counselors on site. The county health service did send a doctor and a nurse once or twice each year to give inoculations and remind us that flies liked visiting our outhouses before walking around on our faces. The teacher's salary and the electric light bill were the only outlays for daily operation. And if cost comparisons didn't decide the issue, the rugged landscape did. A school bus could travel the length of Kings Creek, but it could not make side trips into the hollows. In no hollow was there a road that was passable by a wheeled vehicle, unless that wheeled vehicle was a wagon towed by a good mule. Anyway, when a child had trekked from his up-the-hollow home and out to the Kings Creek Road, he was half-way to school and another half hour of walking wouldn't kill him.

Lower Kings Creek School was closer to my new home at the head of Pace's Branch than were either Middle Kings Creek School or Upper Kings Creek School. Brother Jim and I had a two-mile walk to and from school, and while it wasn't uphill in both directions, it often seemed so, especially in the winter as I slogged along in a heavy pair of arctics—buckle-up rubber galoshes—inside of which my brogans flopped around because the damned arctics were adult-sized and at least two sizes too big, all in order that I might grow into the infernal things and get the use of them for many winters to come. I didn't complain, not after my Uncle Steve had generously provided the boots from the stock in his store, but it was a humbling experience, a little boy in a pair of men's gum boots.

The over-sized boots were just one of the burrs under my saddle that led me to act out in ways that caused my teacher to take a switch to the seat of my overalls seven times in that one school year. I was down-deep pissed off and just didn't know it. I scrapped and scuffled at the slightest provocation. I was always looking, subconsciously no doubt, for a school-yard fight, and larger opponents be damned.

I can guess as to why my behavior went suddenly to Hell—I had been uprooted in a single day and sent away from my mother to live in a forlorn place that nothing in my experience had prepared me for. And then my mother had come to the head of pace's Branch to say a last good-bye, and there followed an unforgettably poignant moment for me.

Jim and I had been with the Calihans just a short while when Mother paid her visit. It was a brief visit and a sad parting, and then she walked away and on down the path. She'd gone out of sight when Bill sent me down to his brother Lloyd's house to collect the latest two-day-old copy of the *Cincinnati Post* newspaper. And there she was again, standing at the far side of the branch, beyond the fenced-in yard at Lloyd Calihan's house and having to shout in order to converse with Lloyd's wife, Nora, who stood at the front edge of the high porch.

I had come through a gate near the back of the house and gone around to the steps and up onto the porch. I could see her, I could hear her, I could wave to her, but I'll never understand why it was that I stood rooted to the porch planks instead of running to her, as I so ached to do. For her part, I can grasp why Mother didn't beckon me to come to her; it would have added pain on top of pain. As a parent, I can see that now

The memory of that painful scene could account some for the anger that dogged me for so long. Lesser reasons might include my new diet, which isn't to suggest at all that Mary Calihan didn't put good hot, plain-but-nutritious, food on the table, and do it at least twice a day. She was a wonder in her little kitchen. Makes me hungry just to think of what she could do there on that small wood-fired "cook stove".

But where were the Moon Pies and the Dr. Peppers? When Jim and I left Roxana, we left behind us the store-bought treats, went cold turkey off junk food. It wasn't as if we were used to a lot of fattening treats with low nutritional value in Roxana—we couldn't afford it—but at the Calihan's we were a four-mile round trip, and that's on foot, away from the closest junk food. Looking back, I have to believe that if we had lived any closer to the soil we'd have been eating it.

And of course I pined for my mother, and it took a long look into the future for me to glimpse any relief for my loneliness. Perhaps that was all I was expressing when I lashed out physically at my school mates.

How angry was I? One cold winter day I and two or three classmates were permitted to sit on the floor around the pot-bellied stove in the back corner of the room while our teacher lectured one of the higher grades. Mr. B called on Cousin Darrell, who sat in the back of the room, to come to the chalk board and write the answer to an exercise. As he came to our outstretched legs, Darrell, always one to tease his younger classmates, kicked my feet aside and said to me, "Move your brogans outta my way, boy." I was stewing with red hot fury, and I pretended to read my Kentucky History book until Darrell turned by the chalkboard to walk toward our teacher, and that's when I closed my book, drew it back past my right ear, and heaved it the length of the room. I saw it was dead-on for the target, and I was seized with dread when my book struck Darrell flush in the face and peeled a bit of skin from the bridge of his nose.

A hush fell over the room, and mouths gaped in stunned disbelief. Mr. B, sweet-natured Mr. B, eventually unclenched his jaws enough to yell at me. "Young man, you just take yourself out by the creek bank and cut a good switch. Then march yourself back in here for your whipping." Darrell was positioned behind Mr. B and grinning as a tiny streak of blood trickled down his nose. Whether he'd meant to or not, Darrell had set me up good, and now he who'd gotten whippings enough of his own had only to stand smugly by and watch as I got mine.

I didn't know that I was just generally an angry child; I lacked the inner awareness to reflect on why I fought and got whippings. The anger came quickly, was acted upon, and then it was gone, so I think I was for the most part fairly happy and not much concerned with why I fought.

Sterling Calihan, one of Bill Calihan's several grandnephews who lived on Pace's Branch, was a classmate. I don't think Sterling had a mean bone in his body, but one day out on the playground I had done something to aggravate him in the extreme. He was older and bigger than me, but he wasn't as slow or clumsy as I might have wished, so I was fleeing for my life. I dodged around the pine-sapling basketball goal-post at the near end of the dirt court and tried to elude Sterling by cutting through the recess brawl that passed for a game of basketball.

Sterling was angrier than I would have thought him capable; he was huffing loudly and gaining ground as we neared the far goalpost. What possessed me to do it I don't know, but in full stride I hooked the knotty goal post with my left hand and made a fist of my right, then, with the added momentum of that swinging pivot, my small fist met Sterling's mouth with a resounding smack.

Maybe the normally placid Sterling was shocked at the turn of events, or maybe he just decided that killing me wasn't worth the trouble. In any event, he desisted and walked sullenly away. But, as I was to learn before school let out, old Sterling wasn't through with me. He and his brother, Jasper, would be laying for me and Jim as we trudged warily along the path up Pace's Branch. They'd be lying in ambush for us, hidden in the shadows, waiting patiently and giving us plenty time to stew and worry.

It would go one of two time-honored ways. They would gather piles of creek stones and wait to attack from behind the bushes, or they'd stand with arms crossed and block our way and say, "We just dare you to walk past us. We, by God, double-dare you."

Those leather-tough Calihan brothers could have massacred me and Jim, but, bless their good country hearts, they had pity for two orphans, two boys who didn't have a daddy like their daddy, who was a section hand on the L & N Railroad, a daddy who though he might be flying a little high when he arrived home late on payday, was still a daddy they could depend on to bring home the candy and soda pop.

I was better behaved during the following school year—mainly because we had a new teacher. Mr. B had been easy-going and probably hated to give whippings, but the new man, Mr. I., didn't shy away from whippings, and when he gave one it was with a stout switch, and he laid it on hard. I witnessed one such thrashing, feeling great pity for the victim, and I decided right then that if I was provoked I'd just wait and see if the matter was worth pursuing when school let out and both parties were away from school grounds. That worked well enough that I don't recall ever going home with red stripes across my butt. Nor do I recall being in any fights at all that year, at school or any other place, but not remembering a fight may only be because I didn't get whipped for it.

I was too easily provoked by my male classmates, but girls were a different matter. One pretty little blonde-headed girl, for all I could imagine about her glamorous life away from school, might have been a princess. Priscilla was so well groomed, and to top it all, she wore a different clean dress every day of the week. She wore white anklets and black patent leather shoes that had a strap across each of her dainty feet. Maybe I was precocious in my sensual imaginings, for I fantasized about Priscilla in a silky pink chemise, not that I knew a chemise from a printed feed sack with arm holes, but I conceived it just the same, with perhaps a nudge from the lingerie pages of a Sears and Roebuck catalog.

Mail-order catalogs were my encyclopedia; the goods in their pages gave me some idea of what others in the world were doing. I was pretty sure they weren't milking cows before breakfast, going to bed at dusk, and missing their mommas.

Gone on the morning train.

11 All Aboard

After school let out in the spring of 1947 Jim and I got a summer reprieve from Pace's Branch. Mother sent word that we were to come visit her in Lexington. I could throw down the hoe, which I didn't much like anyway because I didn't use it to suit Mary Calihan. She and Jim were good at hoeing corn, but I stunk at it. They'd finish hoeing one hill of corn, step to the next one and, reaching far into the balk[7] they'd pull the hoe blade smoothly toward the cluster of two or three stalks that comprised a "hill", skimming away the weeds and at the same time mounding the loosened soil around the base of the stalks. They always stayed well ahead of me, thereby trashing[8] me with the crap they drug from their balk into mine. But since I didn't have any quarrel with weeds, I left the balk alone and just stirred the dirt for a few inches around each hill and called it properly hoed. When the corn had tasseled out it all looked about the same to me anyway, and come harvest time who could prove that the nubbins[9] came from corn stalks I'd hoed?

---

[7] **Balk:** For row crops, such as corn, the balk is the strip of earth that separates any two rows. In hillside farming it was critical to leave walking space between rows to allow for manual cultivation and harvesting.

[8] **Trashing:** The slow hoer who worked downhill from and behind a faster hoer often found his balk littered with weeds and debris. The faster worker had "trashed" him.

[9] **Nubbin:** A stunted or half-formed ear of corn.

We were going to see Mother in Lexington and stay a few weeks until school started up again. The thought pleased me greatly, especially since it meant I wouldn't be around to help with "laying by" the corn, giving it that one final hoeing before taking a break until harvest time.

On the eve of our departure day, we walked the two miles to Roxana and there spent the night with our Uncle Steve Whitaker, who now ran the store that Uncle Isaac Hogg had once run. Steve, like Isaac, had a wife named Gladys, but Steve's Gladys wasn't local, she was from Michigan. She was a trouper, and I suppose it was out of an abiding love for Uncle Steve that she adapted to Roxana without any lasting signs of culture shock. She was, and still is, a real sweetheart, and she must have had a soft spot for two little holler rats, because she cooked for us that day like she was cooking for a whole boarding house.

She stuffed us with chicken and dumplings and home-canned green beans and sweet corn, and then she brought out homemade pie with ice cream. Uncle Steve was all hearty bonhomie, encouraging us to eat until we could eat no more. An hour or so after supper he brought a roll-away bed from the living quarters, situated it behind the back counter of the store, and opened it out flat for us. The mattress was thin, and the supporting cross-bars felt to my back like I was lying across a railroad track; it wasn't what we were used to sleeping on at the Calihan's house, which was one ticking[10] stuffed with the feathers Mary had plucked from all manner of barnyard fowl, and beneath that cloud of softness, another tick stuffed with dried corn shucks. But, drugged as we were by the heavy meal, sleep soon overcame all obstacles, including our keen anticipation of the train ride we'd take in the morning.

I'd never before seen the inside of an L & N Railroad passenger car, not the entirety of one, just fleeting glimpses from outside on the ground. As the conductor helped me mount to the platform and I got my first glimpse, I was much taken by the richly appointed car I would be riding in. Green mohair upholstery on seats supported by heavy iron frames, armrests atop end brackets wrought in a baroque design, gleaming wood panels, and all of it under the soft light cast by large white globes along the recessed ceiling. The scene stuck somewhere in

---

[10] **Ticking**, or tick, is what one calls the mattress-sized sack that holds the feathers for a featherbed. The fabric is usually blue-striped closely-woven cotton or linen.

the back of my mind, and decades later it influenced how I was to refinish an antique oak ice box. The refinished box has a rich grain under the mellow patina of Minwax Polyurethane. I used linseed oil and pumice to buff the pitted nickel coating on the hardware and was surprised at how easily the nickel finish came off to reveal gleaming brass.

I suppose any handy-person could refinish the outside of a wooden box, but I doubt that many had an easy means to cover the inside in green velvet. Through a friend and neighbor I had the use of a patented new process called Velvetex, and now the lining that was once just galvanized tin has a velvety-to-the-touch deep green coating. It all reflects perhaps more than just my memories of that first train ride; it may lean some on how enamored I've long been of the plush décor in the private rail cars that a hundred or more years ago carried the great robber baron industrialists across our land. The refinished ice box resides now with a beloved young relative, where I see it from time to time and am taken sweetly back to the time I travelled in a style fit for a mogul.

Our rail carriage had just a few passengers, as not many had boarded at any of the few small stops between McRoberts, the starting point for that morning's run, and Roxana. Jim and I each had our own seat. The train barely got rolling good before it slowed and stopped at Blackey. I'd been to Blackey only once before, and that was to be fitted with a pair of Star Brand lace-up brogans at my Uncle Vernon Whitaker's little store. Granddaddy Jim Whitaker was high on that particular brand of shoes, probably because they wore well and could be half-soled and passed down from the original wearer to a younger brother.

Many families had their own cast iron cobbler's "last" for the purpose of mending shoes. Granddaddy's last was of three pieces; a base that was nailed to the floor, a stand to position the top piece at a convenient working height, and, at the top of the stand, a foot-shaped piece of iron to fit inside an upturned shoe. The family cobbler, whoever got that prized job, would replace old worn heels and nail a half-sole over what remained of the shoe bottoms. Each steel brad, as it was hammered through the leather, would strike against the iron last and the sharp point would be turned back into the sole where it wouldn't injure the wearer's foot. It always gave me a feeling of confidence to be wearing new half-soles and heels and have a fresh pair of laces.

We'd been riding along, me in the seat in front of Jim's and each of us leaning our head against the window to talk back and forth through the space between my seat-back and the window. All the turning back and forth to share our observations was distracting us from the sightseeing itself, but we looked around inside the car and copied what some other passengers were doing and created our own comfortable little booth by pushing one seat-back opposite its normal position so that we'd ride facing each other. We changed places from time to time so the same one wasn't always looking at the houses and fields and river pools we'd just clickety-clacked past.

When it was my turn to look ahead instead of back, I'd fix my gaze toward the engine and, more specifically, on the big rod that pumped rapidly back and forth between the cylinder and the big drive wheels. The rod connected near the outer edge of the drive wheel and was counterweighted by a crescent-shaped slab of steel inside the wheel's arc exactly opposite the rod connection. Horizontal motion became circular motion as the rod went back and forth and the wheel went smoothly round and round, instead of shaking the apparatus to pieces.

From time to time the track would straighten for a short distance and the engine would draw back until it was in line with the cars behind it, until finally the engine was blocked from my view and I'd be content to study instead every house or shack, every automobile or truck, every derelict piece of rusty farm equipment that came into view for a few seconds and then was gone.

About four hours into our journey, after stopping at Winchester, we had just twenty miles further to go, and no more stops before Lexington. We were well out of the valley of the North Fork of the Kentucky River and onto a fairly straight section of track for a change, where the locomotive could snort like the beast it was and run the way God intended it to run. With the hills behind us, the scene out the window stretched out across the gently rolling hills of the outer Bluegrass. White fences flashed past, and beyond them I saw fat cattle grazing, and here and there were horses of a type I'd never before seen. They appeared to be full grown and yet not nearly as heavy as the horses I'd seen pulling sleds, wagons, or plows back in the hills. These sleek animals, Thoroughbreds, as I was to learn, weren't even as big as Chet Mitchell's Tennessee Walking Horse. How light on their feet they seemed when suddenly one would swing its head and gallop away from the others.

The grass seemed to go on forever, and the sky was so incredibly broad. Daylight must last twice as long here as it did up Pace's

Branch. I carry a mental picture, a snapshot so seemingly mundane that the only significance I can think to attribute to it is that it is simply a tab on a page of my memories. On a gentle grassy slope in a pasture bordered by white board fencing sits a feeder, a white-washed structure about the size of a roadside hut where children shelter while awaiting their school bus, just a gabled roof on two uprights, sheltering two feed boxes. That's what I see when I think back on the day I first came to see how different were two worlds that lay so close by each other. That bucolic scene is an indelible sign post in my memory and one of several by which I find my way back to who I was back then.

I don't remember anything of what I saw as the train rolled slowly through Lexington's eastern suburbs, nothing, in fact, until we stopped behind the Union Station Depot. We disembarked and were directed to the gate leading into the waiting area. As we passed by the engine, it hissed and sighed, and I hung back some to study the running gear and marvel at the size of the drive wheels, all taller than me, and wonder why the whole great mass of steel didn't just sink right through the steel rails and crossties until only the boiler and cab remained above ground.

As for the interior of the Union Station, I could not back then compare it to a cathedral, but I'm reasonably sure that what I felt was akin to what a tourist of today must feel upon entering the central nave of St. Peter's Basilica in Rome. Our footsteps echoed off the domed ceiling that seemed to soar a hundred feet overhead. It was an awful lot of hollowed out space just to serve the traveler. The ticket agents and the offices of other railroad people were along the perimeter, and it seemed a long walk from one to the other. I recall the blind news agent at a stand immediately inside the gate; he had enough comic books and sweet snacks to do business for a year back in Roxana.

Mother waited inside the station to welcome us. After the hugs, we headed for the nearest bus stop. On exiting Union Station toward East Main Street, we followed a sidewalk that curved around a sunken garden, and in the center of the garden was a fountain; it was set off by many shrubs and flowers. At the bus stop I gazed back at the magnificent facade, the central gable flanked by towering spires, each topped by an American flag. What a grand sight it was. And it's long since gone, a victim of Urban Renewal, which grieved me at the time, as I thought it to be the unnecessary destruction of a sight worth holding onto.

Illustration by Jody

Lexington's Union Station Depot

Across Main Street was the Strand Theater. The Strand was one of Lexington's seven movie houses at the time and was what you might call a blue-collar place. I don't know what was playing the first time I laid eyes on it, but with what I was to learn about the Strand, I'm sure the marquee announced a couple of "B" movies, perhaps Roy Rogers in a Republic Pictures film shot in *Trucolor*, a color process that looked a little washed-out compared to a film done in Technicolor. The second feature was most likely a black-and-white whodunit featuring actors who weren't on Hollywood's "A" list and who were unlikely to make it into the pages of *Photoplay* Magazine. At the time I knew it was a place I'd come back to, as I did a couple of years later, after I'd returned to Lexington to stay.

I had no idea where in Lexington my mother was living, but she said we needed to catch a bus going west. We crossed Main and then crossed Walnut Street to the bus stop in front of Bradley's Drug Store. Across Main Street from us stood a most imposing structure, almost as magnificent as the train depot. It was the Lafayette Hotel. It was said to be a ten story building, but from counting the rows of windows it looked to be much taller.

A few yards east of the Lafayette the big flashy marquee of the Kentucky Theater shaded the sidewalk all the way to the curb. The Kentucky was the finest movie house in town, the place where the men of the University of Kentucky took their dates to see the films of Doris Day and Rock Hudson, the plots of which all turned on miscommunication and sexual frustration and featured twin beds in all the bedroom scenes.

The bus we boarded was a dull red and yellow, and I was puzzled to read on the outside that it was operated by the Lexington *Railway* System. It didn't resemble a train and I saw no tracks, just big rubber tires on a blacktop-paved street. I learned some years later that this same company had for many years operated streetcars throughout the city and that the name was a carryover. Not all the old tracks had been paved over yet, however, and after I'd moved to Lexington and become a frequent bus rider I got to see a section of track on Chestnut Street in the northeast part of Lexington where the residents were mostly African-American and most likely didn't often see their streets repaired or repaved.

The bus hove into sight then slowed to a nose-down stop before settling back on its suspension system. The accordion doors folded back with a gushing hiss and we stepped aboard, but we had to wait at the top step as Mother dropped three tokens into what resembled a parking meter on a stand that was waist high. I was surprised to see that the driver was female. That is another of the scenes that remain finely etched in my memory. A stout fortyish woman, the driver reached her left hand across the big steering wheel to swing away from the curb, and with her right hand she hauled back on the long gear shifter while simultaneously leaning back to glance in her side mirror. I'd have been happy to ride the route all the way around, just so I could sit and admire how confidently she handled that big rumbling machine.

Some years later I learned that the woman bus driver was the equivalent of Rosie the Riveter, a holdover from wartime when, thanks to the shortage of able-bodied men, women broke through, albeit temporarily, the gender barriers in the workplace. When I returned to Lexington a year or so later all the lady bus drivers had vanished, their places taken, one supposes, by returning servicemen.

At west Main and Broadway we transferred to another bus whose sign above the windshield said "Versailles Rd." Along Broadway just two blocks south of Main we passed only residences, all old-looking red brick of two stories with white gingerbread trim. That pattern held until we turned west on High Street, where, to judge by the tiny bare yards and peeling paint, began a section of Old Lexington that you won't see in travel brochures from that time. It wasn't a slum, not at all, just tired-looking old buildings waiting for the time when yuppie couples and imaginative entrepreneurs would move in and do their makeovers, which by and large they've done in recent years, and to pleasing effect, for a part of the city within a six-block radius of the intersection of Main and Limestone Streets.

I'd just as soon not have seen Irishtown, the slum whose name I couldn't grasp the meaning of at the time. On a few acres of low-lying land that was crossed over by a viaduct sat small dwellings crowded together side by side. To the immediate front of each small dwelling was a street, sometimes paved but often not, and close behind each house was the back of another house. Conditions here looked to me to be some worse than in Roxana, where even the poorest home generally had a shade tree or two, a well that gave fresh drinking water, and space enough around it that the privy didn't stand in the shadow of the house. It looked to me that any resident of Irishtown would necessarily always be downwind of someone's privy.

Irishtown and nearby Davis Bottom are gone now, having been razed and replaced by modern streets and attractive housing during Lexington's push for Urban Renewal in the 1970s.

Our bus cleared the west end of the viaduct and we were away from the slum and looking out at rows of long, low, corrugated steel buildings, some of the many tobacco warehouses that the R. J. Reynolds Tobacco Company had placed in various parts of Lexington.

West High Street became Versailles Road, the sights became greatly more welcoming, and in a few blocks we were passing only well-tended residences. At the backs of deep lawns sat stately brick homes of two and three stories, and dotted among them were white frame houses with dark green shutters. Where the front yard elevations were noticeably higher than the sidewalk, the sidewalk was abutted by retaining walls of cut stone.

We were just a few blocks into this hospitable-looking neighborhood when mother reached up and gave a pull on the cord that ran the length of the bus. A buzzer sounded and the driver brought the bus to a stop for us to disembark. As the bus pulled away we waited for traffic to clear on the four-lane highway, a road that certain detractors of former Governor Happy Chandler claimed he'd had built as his personal driveway to carry him with speed and comfort from his home in Versailles to downtown Lexington.

Our destination turned out to be Hunt's Tourist Home, directly across the road from the bus stop. With two stories plus an attic and a steeply-gabled roof, the red brick structure looked as solid as a fortress. Mother opened the front door without knocking and the three of us entered the foyer and climbed a long stairway to her small furnished apartment on the second floor.

The place was a nice big home in a suburban neighborhood, a neighborhood that lacked just about everything that a boy might find interesting. There was zilch for amusement. But at least we didn't have to feed and water livestock or milk two cows morning and night, and we'd dodged a bullet inasmuch as there was no corn to be hoed. I won't get on a pity pot about an eight-year-old boy having to hoe corn, not when I see on my TV that children in the Third World labor harder and longer every day and that so very many of them do it with little hope of ever being free of their yoke. We were far from being oppressed, my brother and me, for we'd had the good fortune, after all, to be born in a land with few institutional barriers between a resourceful white citizen and material rewards.

Mother occasionally gave us each a nickel to spend for ice cream at a nearby restaurant, just a couple of blocks toward town. It was great ice cream, *French Bauer*, I think. Any time I came into a nickel, it weighed heavily in my pocket, burning a hole, as the saying goes, until I was permitted to spend it. I can see myself so clearly the time I threw a nickel as far as I could heave it, into the tall weeds and gone.

I guess my mother thought by giving me a nickel she was providing me something to look forward to. And that was true enough, or truer, I imagine, than she bargained for. No, I couldn't go just then to the ice cream place; I'd just have to wait. I went down the stairs and out on the lawn, and there I seethed and stomped, back and forth, back and forth, until I could take it no more. In a fit of stammering petulance, with tears leaking down my cheeks and the nickel in my throwing hand, I ran a few steps and launched that nickel into the shrubbery at the far side of the adjoining lawn. Good, I thought, you sonofabitching useless damn nickel. Still the deep-down angry child, once again I was acting out.

The summer weeks fled past in a blur, and it came time to board the train for our trip back to Roxana. I recall that return train ride more sharply than anything we did in Lexington. Soon after the train left Lexington, we raised the windows by our seats and leaned our faces into the wind, and from time to time we'd rub a cinder from our eyes. We went to explore the car and discovered at one end a smoking lounge, and in that lounge we spied a thick Sears and Roebuck catalog. And no adult hanging about to discourage the notion it inspired in us.

We leaned out the window and peered hopefully ahead until finally we hit a curve and could see in the distance a bridge, a very high bridge, just what we needed. Actually it wasn't a bridge; it was a trestle that rose what seemed like 200 feet above a small stream. Being a trestle, it supported the tracks entirely from below, and there was nothing higher than the tracks to obstruct our view as we approached our target. We waited until we saw far below us a field of dense green weeds that stretched a good ways to the banks of the river. "Bombs away," we said not too loudly, and dropped the catalog. It didn't tumble through the air, but stayed flat and spun lazily round and round, it's initial forward momentum serving to keep it well within sight until it slammed into the weeds, a scant couple of yards short of the river that had been our target. The high-five hadn't yet been invented, so we probably just grinned at each other.

Back home on the evening train.

12   Cowboys and Haints

The only movie I got to see in my entire first nine years was one time when my family took the train to Hazard, Kentucky. I remember but a single scene, and it may have been from a Newsreel, because it was gruesome in the extreme. A Japanese woman, clad only in a half-slip and clasping her arms across her breasts, steps into space from the edge of a high cliff and plunges to her death. We know now that Japanese civilians on the island of Okinawa in World War II committed suicide in shocking numbers because they were ordered by the Japanese Imperial Army to kill themselves rather than fall into the clutches of the U.S. marines that Japanese propaganda portrayed as heathen devils.

On returning to Pace's Branch from our visit to Lexington, I didn't know just how ready I was to watch a movie when we heard the exciting news that Hays Stamper had built a "show house" up on Kings Creek. Our friends at Lower Kings Creek School exulted at the prospect of seeing Hoot Gibson, Johnny Mack Brown, Ken Maynard, Bob Steele, and other cowboy actors in that golden era of "B" westerns. But I was only to hear my friends' excited jabbering about them, and about the Three Stooges, whoever they were, and I was never to see any of them on the small screen at Hays Stamper's Show House.

Jim and I lived at the head of Pace's Branch, a good two mile walk from the cinema capitol of southwest Letcher County, two very spooky miles when darkness fell upon the tree-shrouded path.

Even in daylight one had to pay attention to the trip hazards presented by jutting stones and roots that awaited just inches from the path that was crooked as a snake and not much wider, and if the ground was wet there was no shortage of slippery slopes. Augmenting all these sound reasons not to travel the path at night was the possibility that if we did so we would be accosted by a haint[11]. Bill Calihan said so, though not as a direct warning. No, old Bill just told us a tale of "a feller" who'd had a harrowing experience and lived to tell about it and also to mend his ways in the hope of never again being seized by such terror.

This unfortunate had been on a toot and was riding his old mule up the dark hollow toward home, leaving it to his sure-footed old friend to find and follow the path by his own good instincts. The drunken fellow was humming a tune and paying no attention to the low tree branches that swatted him in the face, when suddenly the mule did a stutter step that jolted his rider from his dozy reverie. Puzzled but not alarmed, the fellow shrugged and sank again into a mumbling doze, only to be shocked awake by a scream that split the dead silence of the night. Coming as nearly awake as one in his condition could, he questioned for a second whether he might be in his own bed and experiencing a nightmare. But two strong arms squeezing him about the waist settled his thinking on that matter. He gasped as he felt the strength drain from his body, and sobbing and praying, and heedless of whatever danger might lay ahead in the inky darkness, he kicked his heels into the flanks of his steed, hoping for a brisk gallop. The old mule gave him a few quick steps and then wisely fell back into what was a sensible gait for the conditions. The rider again clamped his heels hard into the brute's flanks, and on getting no response at all this time, he knew to the bottom of his soul that tonight he would certainly die.

Some very long minutes later, panting hard and near to fainting, the now mostly sober rider was slow to believe it when he no longer felt the chilly embrace of the haint. Looking neither left nor right and fearful of knowing what might be behind him, the man rode on home. There he dismounted, and on his knees he kissed the ground and promised, "Oh, lord, I ain't never in my life gonna sin no more, ner nevermore on this earth drink no likker ever agin."

---

[11] **Haints** to some may be ghosts or spirits of the dead, but on Pace's Branch a haint was more than a spirit. An angry haint could do a body some real hurt.

Go to the picture show? Me and Jim? After learning of the Pace's Branch Haint? Hell, no. Not if Tom Mix was fighting King Kong in the Streets of Laredo. Well, maybe, if it was a matinee show that began right soon after breakfast.

We never saw a single picture show at Hays Stamper's Show House, but Jim and I were most fortunate in getting to see a live music show there.

Talk of the Stanley Brothers' coming appearance at Stamper's Show House consumed us for a few days. Neither we nor, I dare say, the Stanley Brothers themselves, could know of the path to musical fame that lay ahead for this duo who would capture the soul of Appalachian music and endear themselves to a worldwide audience decades before the Coen Brothers released their movie, *O Brother, Where Art Thou?*, in which the critically-acclaimed soundtrack featured the Stanleys.

The news went up every hollow, until everyone spoke in tones of wonderment about an "electric" mandolin that Pewee Lambert would be playing at the big show. An electric mandolin, huh? I'd seen electric lights, and since electricity had made its way to my Granny's house, I'd seen her oscillating electric fan that she was so pleased and grateful to sit in front of on a hot summer day, but I couldn't begin to picture what an electric mandolin might do; I reckoned it would probably strum itself.

On a weekend visit when we stayed over with Aunt Gladys and Uncle Isaac, he broke the big news that Jim and I would accompany their little family when they went to the show. I looked forward to riding in Uncle Isaac's fine new automobile, a blue 1948 Chevy Fleetline Sedan, all sleek and aerodynamic with headlights and fenders integrated into the body lines. That car was a Kings Creek wonder, so much leaner and faster looking than the old black clunkers on which the bolted-on fenders and all the exterior lights stuck out like afterthoughts.

It was a short ride up Kings Creek to Stamper's show House. Uncle Isaac parked his car and we got out in time to see Carter and Ralph Stanley as they drove up in a shiny new Kaiser automobile—or it may have been a Frazer, I saw so few cars of any make, and those two always seemed to resemble each other. I don't recall what color that sexy-looking car was, but it wasn't black like so many of the other cars that had showed up.

The show house itself was a sturdy little board-and-batten frame building made of unpainted lumber that looked to be fresh from the sawmill. Inside were wooden benches arranged like church pews, except these were low to the floor and had no backrests.

The Stanley's, on the other hand, put on some personal style that reflected pride in who they were and what they were about. Silver-gray Stetson hats, summery-looking short-sleeved shirts, light gray gabardine slacks, and on their feet were leather sandals. What in the world! I had to be told what they were, these sandals, "like what Jesus wore, honey; you know, back in Bible times."

The brothers set their microphones up front in the center of the stage portion of the room, on the floor and level with the audience, perhaps six feet away from the occupants of the first row. The sidemen, on mandolin, fiddle, and stand-up bass, were on the wings.

I recall two of the songs they performed, *White Dove* and *Sweeter than the Flowers*, both mournful tunes of loss and longing. And I remember the antics of "Cousin Winesap", the bass player in the clown getup that was a mandatory part of all similar groups of the time.

Cousin Winesap: Why'd the chicken cross the road?

Carter Stanley: You got me, Cousin.

Cousin Winesap: To git to 'tother side.

(Uproarious laughter)

Winesap: Why does Uncle Sam wear red, white, and blue suspenders?

Carter: To show he's patriotic?

Winesap: Naw, to hold his britches up.

(More laughter)

In later years, sometime after Carter died in 1966, as the Stanley Brothers came to be recognized and honored for the musical pioneers they were, I was to realize what a seminal event their Kings Creek performance had been for me.

In the spring of 1974 or 1975 I was at a Kmart in Versailles, Kentucky buying some fishing gear, and I'd already checked out when my eye was caught by a display of cassette tapes that were going for just one or two dollars. I already owned a few vinyl LPs by Bluegrass artists, but I had none by the Stanley Brothers. And there it was in the top row, Carter and Ralph against a red background with the words "16 greatest hits", as though they'd known I'd be back someday. I picked up the cassette and read the titles on the back; most were still familiar to me.

That cassette tape led me to make a number of improvements in how I listened to my favorite kind of music. I ordered a Heathkit component stereo system that arrived as a few empty cabinets and a great many tiny electronic components. I commandeered the living room and arrayed all the components, and then I commenced soldering thing "A" to thing "B", and when I had it fully assembled a miracle occurred. I plugged the FM receiver into the amplifier, and when I plugged the amplifier into the wall outlet and turned it on, it played; it gave out sound, the sound of music. I, who knew nothing at all about electronics, should have framed the printed instructions; they were so complete, absolutely faultless. I was thrilled with my sound, and ten watts of "Continuous Power" per channel produced quite enough volume, and never mind what audiophiles demand today; any more might have been too much. Any louder and I'd have risked having a musically untutored neighbor yell at our house, "Turn down that damn banjo noise," and our friendship might have suffered.

There was more than just pies at pie suppers.

13   Pie Suppers an' Fightin'

In the mid-1940s a few homes in Roxana had electricity, but some families still powered their radios with a six-volt car battery. If they kept it charged, they could hear the news of the day from Edward R. Murrow or Gabriel Heatter, and listen to soap operas, and on Saturday nights they'd gather around the big console and hear Roy Acuff, Minnie Pearl, and other old friends on the *Grand Ole Opry* from Station WSM in Nashville. The sound came and went, wavering up and down in response to changing atmospheric conditions. We made some improvement in the reception by running a grounding wire out through a window and attaching it to a metal stake that was driven deep into the ground. For optimal electrical grounding we kept the earth around our "aerial" thoroughly dampened by pouring a bucket of water on it every day or so.

Our sole form of electronic entertainment was to sit in the living room and listen to the radio. Mother might sew or crochet, and others of us might work a jigsaw puzzle while we listened to songs or to half-hour dramas, like *Boston Blackie*, or comedies, like *Amos 'n' Andy*, but radio listening was generally a private family activity. After a long fall and winter of near hibernation, we craved to come together with our neighbors and blow off some steam from time to time, and that drove us to plan social events that included the whole community in the fun.

"Pie Suppers" were not-to-be-missed occasions that featured live music and an auction. The pie auction was a once-a-year opportunity for a fellow to sweeten his chances with a girl he'd had his eye on by bidding an exorbitant amount for the pie she'd made for the occasion.

If he dug deep into his pockets and held his ground against other bidders he got the pie, either a cream pie piled high with toasted meringue, or a fruit pie with a crispy lattice top crust, and, what was even better, he enjoyed the exclusive company of the pie's creator as they sat by themselves and shared the treat. For certain young swains it was worth the money and worth waiting a year, if they could meet that certain someone. It bypassed all potential barriers including, for the moment at least, other possible suitors for that same delicate hand.

My Uncle Burnett Hogg, older brother to my late father, made himself available for the role of auctioneer. He was a bluff and hearty character, full of tales and good humor and never lacking for confidence in any social situation. He was ever dedicated to the task of auctioning off pies, needling and cajoling the young men to part with their last dime or else skulk away and be known ever after for their tight grip on a nickel.

Our county was legally dry, meaning that the preachers and bootleggers craftily encouraged the prohibition of alcohol sales, which in turn allowed the preachers to proclaim that God's work had been done and the bootleggers to retain their exclusive hold on the underground market for strong spirits.

So it was that the men, not all of them, but still a goodly number, would sidle away from the pie supper proceedings and steal out to where they'd stashed their pint, and it was almost always a pint, for the pint was the bottle size favored by the bootleggers. A pint of Four Roses fit into a jacket pocket and had the kick to keep a man mellow for the duration of a pie supper or a dance party.

Some historical society would do well to erect a marker where once stood the Lower Kings Creek school house and honor it as the site of the "Great Pie Supper Battle". As a memorable occasion, this debacle had it all, live music and pies galore, all so lovingly made, and all to be paid for in the name of charity, and all of it punctuated by a grand melee of fist-fighting. And lastly, a story they could all laugh about as they mended relations in the days that followed, the story of a team of affable young ruffians who stole the night without throwing a punch.

Uncle Burnett, in his comic turn as master of ceremonies, jollied and teased the crowd into a state of high expectation, but it was too soon yet to begin auctioning off the pies. He'd wait a while longer and give the slow starters time to duck out for another slug or two of the stuff that might nerve up a henpecked husband to where he'd ignore his gimlet-eyed "old woman" and bid the grocery money for a pie that had been touched by hands that he secretly longed to hold in his own.

Uncle B had the band assemble in front of the chalkboard and begin playing. The *ad hoc* group of musicians was composed of four friends playing guitar, fiddle, banjo, and stand-up bass. Three of the musicians were so-so, but the banjo player, whom I won't name, was not quite up to so-so. He was a beginner on the instrument, and it showed. The crowd suffered along with his stumbling efforts until one man, a loud mouth at the best of times and louder still now that he was on the way to being properly drunk, called out, "You stink. Sit down and let somebody play that can."

If Earl—we'll call him Earl—couldn't play to suit old Loudmouth, well, he'd, by God, show the heckler just how well he could fight. Amid calls to "Settle down now, boys", Earl, all red in the face, laid his banjo aside and chairs began to slide away from old Loudmouth, making room for the fight that might after all be more entertaining than the music.

The crowd quickly took sides, with brothers, cousins, and uncles lining up to join the fray. Who threw the first punch is a question that was never settled among the antagonists, but hackles were raised all around and, with the suddenness of two dogs rising on their hind legs to snap and snarl over a bone, Earl and his heckler came crashing together. Flailing away at each other, they fell to the floor in a sweaty embrace, gouging and biting, while all around them their respective male kinfolks, and one or two females, joined in the fun.

Was anyone watching the cloakroom where the pies were lined up on the shelves awaiting the big auction? Yes, as a matter of fact, three of my clever first cousins, Porter, Duncan, and Darrell, along with both my older brothers, Manfred and Jim, were keeping an eye on the pies, as they'd been doing all evening, hoping for just such an opportunity.

While all eyes were on the sprawling melee, Duncan, the rangiest of the three, pulled Jim by the hand as they eased through the cloakroom door and closed it behind them. The jalousie windows were high in the wall, so Duncan pushed a table against that wall and boosted Jim up onto it. Duncan handed the pies up to Jim; Jim poked the pies out through the window and let them fall; outside were the pie catchers, Manfred, Porter, and Darrell.

How best to conceal all those pies? The answer: eat all you can, forget the rest, and then hide yourself and your bulging belly until it no longer stuck out as evidence of your crime.

I don't know how things wound down that long-ago evening, but if events followed their normal course, the matter was allowed to subside without having the law come meddling in. You didn't go "lawing" somebody just because you got a busted nose and some contusions in a fair fight. Revenge was a personal matter and not to be bought through the agency of a lawsuit. A bitter loser could be counted on for some time afterward to seize on any chance to blackguard the fellow who "wouldn't have whupped me 'thout he sucker punched me, the low down sumbitch bastard."

There was little of festering rancor in the days following the pie supper fight, and it would later be recalled as not exactly family fare but still a friendly sort of brawl, a sprawling mess around which there were enough sober people to prevent any serious maiming. A brawl like this one might be big, but you could say there was some safety in numbers. A private fight, on the other hand, could be a serious affair, like it was with the donnybrook that took place in a Roxana storeroom during a game of stud poker.

Four young men, all of them single, sinewy, and, as was to be proved, unschooled in anger management, sat facing each other across an upturned cardboard box on which the cards were dealt. Their women stood around the table, outwardly chatty, but inwardly celebrating, or fretting furiously, as luck shifted, favorably or cruelly.

The players were four friends, bonded by mutual distrust and past exploits that caused some in the community to look askance at the lot of them. Amid the loud laughter and drinking, DJ was losing badly. His woman stood clasping in her hand a Bull Durham tobacco sack, the kind with a drawstring closure, and now it was near to empty, the stake gone, most of it into the pockets of Zack G.

Zack must have been drunk, else he would have seen or felt it when DJ surreptitiously eased a firecracker into the top of his shoe and set a match to the fuse.

The firecracker went off with a loud report, cards flew into the air, the stench of burnt powder filled the room, and much screeching and loud swearing ensued. Zack, in obvious pain, hopped around on one foot for a bit and then lunged for DJ, and they fell to the floor punching and kicking, clawing and gouging, Zack bent on maiming his tormentor, DJ fighting for his life.

It was an ugly fight, for sure, but as neither combatant resorted to gun or knife, or even brass knuckles, the animosity would fade, in parallel with the blackened eyes going slowly from deep shades of purple to green highlights, and on into other colorful touches, and finally back to normal, with perhaps a scar or two, the architect of which would studiously avoid noticing when eventually the parties chanced to meet again.

Why, one may ask, did the Roxana men and boys turn so quickly to settle matters with fists or, on occasion, with deadly weapons? For an answer to that question I'll consult a not terribly renowned amateur cultural anthropologist, namely me.

It's generally true that mountain men were quick to take offence. It's true that the affronted person could just try to forget about whatever had stuck in his craw, but such pacifists were few among those I knew back then. The choice, then, was between striking out in the heat of the moment or else to plot an ambush for revenge. But, why were these men that way?

I say it was partly owing to their lack of opportunity for settling disagreements in a more civilized manner. The ordinary mountain man with limited formal education and no professional status belonged to two social groups, a family and a neighborhood. He wasn't a Rotarian, a Moose, or an Elk. He belonged to no organized subgroup or institution, except in some instances, a church of some type. He had not the luxury of relishing the time when he could blackball a rival at a lodge meeting, or take him down a peg at the PTA meeting. Poor in material assets, he had little beyond his sense of manly pride. If it's a given that a mountain man of seventy years ago would not overlook a slight and that he demanded satisfaction for an insult, and if it's also true that legal arbiters were generally beyond his means, then what were the options available to him, options that we might reasonably expect him to consider?

He saw himself as very much on his own. So I think a fair fight was to be preferred over sulking and smoldering and putting off the inevitable resolution until it took the form of a cold-blooded act of deep-seated hatred. Under the circumstances of the time, one might argue that fighting was healthy, and that not a few murders, in which for every life ended another life is forever ruined, would have been averted if the warring parties had spent their boiling rancor right there and right then, at Ground Zero.

So, give the mountain man of yore a little credit and allow that but for the custom of fighting, revenge killings might have happened more than the relatively few times they actually did.

Beekeeping the hard way.

14   Earning our Keep

As I've noted elsewhere, our mother didn't pay much out of pocket toward the board bill for Jim and me at the Calihan's house, but still the dear old couple wasn't left with the short end of the stick. My brother and I, at ages 9-12 and 7-10, respectively, were willing workers, and I can say truthfully that Bill, who was already about seventy years of age, never roused himself from his chair at the far end of the porch while we were around to take on any task that needed doing.

In my early adulthood I used to bemoan the fact that I'd been kept away from the "real" world for my first ten years, but for many years now I've been thankful that I was tested early and that I learned to use man-sized tools; I have no doubt that this toughened me in a way that served me in later life—even if my overall childhood experience left some emotional scars.

The two-man crosscut saw is a case in point. If you push a crosscut saw, all you'll accomplish is to wear yourself out. By trial and error we learned the back-and-forth rhythm, in which neither of us pushed but always pulled and then relaxed in that sliver of a second while the other pulled, always allowing the saw itself to dictate the tempo. We learned that some woods were tougher than others. Oak tested and toughened us, but we also got to saw a lot of dead Chestnut that gave itself to the saw's teeth with an ease that led us to see how deep we could cut with each stroke.

Firewood was a basic necessity, and unlike with certain primitive societies we couldn't just walk out and gather fagots off the ground; heating and cooking required a great many more BTUs than could ever be generated from limbs blown down in storms. Mary fired her cook stove with wood, and never with the smoky, stinky coal that their coal bank yielded and that did well enough for the fireplace. And even the fireplace needed dry kindling to get the coal going, plus, Mary's weekly laundry chores used up a fair amount of firewood.

Mary did her laundry outside on a flat piece of ground between the side-yard fence and the shallow branch that flowed past. A big black cauldron hung from a fence rail that was supported by two stout wooden uprights. We dipped buckets into the clear stream and filled the cauldron. Then we carried firewood from the woodshed and built what amounted to a small bonfire beneath the kettle.

When the water reached a rolling boil, Mary shaved homemade lye soap over it. A big yellow cake of lye soap wasn't much for making suds, but it was pretty effective at loosening the dirt from a pair of overalls that had been worn for a week or more. Mary could have made her own lye by leaching water through wood ashes, and in days gone by she probably did, but cans of lye sold cheap at Chet Mitchell's store, which was a four mile round trip that Bill made monthly when he'd throw his old McClellan saddle on Sam and spend a half day getting there and back.

The second important ingredient in lye soap was fat, and this we had in a great plenty, for Mary fried some kind of pork for almost every meal and always saved the grease for making soap.

As the dirty clothes boiled in hot soapy water, Mary poked and prodded them with a wooden paddle, or "battling stick", as it was sometimes called. When the water was discolored enough to suit her, she dipped the garments from the steaming cauldron and dropped them into a washtub where she hand-rubbed them with lye soap and scrubbed them against the ridged surface of a washboard. Then it was on to another tub of clear water for rinsing and wringing by hand, and finally she'd drape the garment across the top of the paling[12] fence to dry.

A mountain farmstead of the time ran pretty much on firewood, and special firewood at that; dead Chestnut wood for kindling, and hardwoods for long burning and good heat output.

---

[12] A **paling** fence may be thought of as a picket fence, but palings are rough and splintery as compared to milled pickets. They were hand-riven by a maul, which is a wooden club, and a froe, which is a long, heavy steel blade attached to an upright wooden handle. The maul was used to pound the froe along the grain of a slab of oak to "rive" a paling from the side of the slab.

We had an abundance of Oak and Hickory, and dead Chestnut trees were still to be found in the late 1940s, some forty years after the blight that began around 1900-1908 and by 1940 had all but wiped out the American Chestnut. The dead chestnut trees, having lost their leaves and every scrap of bark, were silvery sentinels dotting the forested slopes above the Calihan's corn patches, and when kindling ran low, Bill would scan the woods with an old pair of brass-trimmed binoculars and point one out and send me and Jim to fetch it to the wood lot.

We'd harness Sam and clip on the drag chain, and with a double-bitted axe in hand we'd trudge up the hillside. As scrawny as we were, we made the chips fly and took little time felling the smallish tree that Bill had directed us to. We whacked off small limbs and knocked the drag chain hooks into the butt of the tree, and with a down-hill drag Sam had the easy part in getting it down to the wood lot. There we would hammer the drag hooks away from the tree and one of us would lead old Sam to his stall and free him of the harness while the other got out the two-man crosscut saw and made ready to cut the tree into lengths that would fit the firebox of the little kitchen stove. We took pleasure in splitting the chunks, so straight was the grain and so easily did they fly apart when struck with a sharp axe. By felling the tree early in the morning and getting right on to the sawing and splitting, we could show a respectable pile of stove wood by supper time and feel satisfaction for the labor we'd accomplished.

The Tulip Poplar didn't make kindling to compare with Chestnut, but it gave us a goodly portion of our "burning" wood. It was a Poplar tree that came near to taking Jim's head off.

The tree stood at the foot of the hill not far from the house, so Mary came with us when we walked to the back of their small apple orchard. Jim hefted the axe and notched the tree on the uphill side so it would fall in that direction rather than into a nearby gully. We laid the crosscut saw level and commenced sawing through the trunk on the downhill side opposite the felling notch, which ended up doing its job only too well.

At first, the sap in the green wood caused the saw to bind. My brother and I huffed and sweated until finally, as the tree began to lean uphill as we intended, we let go of the saw handles, happy to let gravity finish the job for us. I stood away to one side, but Jim stepped around to stand downhill of the tree, placing himself in what seemed a safe position from which to yell "tim-berrrr" and watch with huge satisfaction as the tree began the long arc of its fall. We waited expectantly for the resounding *whump* of the tree striking the ground, where it would lay quivering for some moments.

With all eyes on the top of the Poplar, no one noticed the growing crack that opened in the top side of the axed-out notch. As the tree passed about forty-five degrees in its arc it picked up speed, and with a loud shriek the butt of a thick slab some ten feet in length swished past Jim's nose so close it had to have brushed his forelock.

Mary gave a soft whistle as though to say, "Whew, lordy child!" We were all three of us shaken, but we grinned our way past the scare, and no one was undone by the close call, but if Jim had stood two inches closer he'd have suffered a broken neck, or a crushed lower jaw, or had all his teeth shattered.

Emergency medical help was so remote from the head of Pace's Branch that the idea never entered our heads. I mean, if one of us sustained a compound fracture of a leg, would we hitch old Sam to the box sled and "rush" the victim to the emergency room? We took what precautions we could, but I submit to you that the hillside farmers of Old Appalachia couldn't dwell on the hazards that awaited them at every turn. If a man survived childhood, and if he lost only a few of his digits throughout his working life, then he could say of himself, "I reckon I'm purty cautious, or just purty damn lucky."

There's a first time for everything, including a first time to die, but you could say that Jim and I never ran out of first times when one or the other of us almost died. Yessir, we wuz real damn lucky.

Shoveling cow shit presented few hazards, except if in order to save your only pair of shoes you waded into it in your bare feet, as Jim and I did in the spring when it was time to manure the Calihan's large vegetable garden. Maybe hookworms can't survive in cow shit and that's why we didn't turn pale and lose our appetites or display other signs of Iron deficiency anemia. If we felt weak or tired, we didn't credit it to anything but hard work.

But why, I wonder, didn't I ever get *trichinosis*? I was qualified. I ate raw pork—smokehouse-cured, but raw just the same—from time to time, and I've since learned that one can ingest the roundworm *Trichinella Spiralis* from raw pork. I learned to like salt-cured side meat, which wasn't bloody raw, but it had never experienced heat in excess of the summer temperatures in the smokehouse. The temperatures inside the smokehouse were probably somewhat warmer than the inside of a live hog, but not nearly warm enough to alter the taste, texture, or composition of the fatty meat, or of whatever organisms that may have dwelt within it. The lean streaks were a rich brown and had a texture a little like beef jerky. Add a raw onion fresh from the garden, a hunk of crusty cornbread and cool buttermilk in a mason jar, and it suited my palate pretty well. Perhaps salt curing made the otherwise raw pork inhospitable for that unseen devil, *Trichinella Spiralis*.

Before going to live with the Calihans I had already contracted and survived almost all of childhood's infectious diseases, and I was lucky in that I didn't have to go through them at the head of Pace's Branch, where Vicks Salve—we'd choke on our pretension were we to call it Vicks "Vaporub"—and Mullein tea were indicated for cough or fever. My mother had nursed me through whooping cough, German measles, scarlet fever, diphtheria, and mumps, all while we lived on Kings Creek in the house I was born in. She wasn't a "granny woman" practiced in the herbal-healing arts, but she didn't spare the Vicks Salve. She'd grease my chest with Vicks and cover it with an old wool sweater that both my sisters had outgrown. The vapors drifted up and helped to keep my nasal passages clear, and that may have been the sole reason Mother slathered it on my chest.

Mary Calihan never practiced any doctoring on me or Jim. She knew how to help a cow to expel a slimy calf that was reluctant to leave its mama's uterus, and she knew what to do when her baby chicks got the "gapes" and were chronically short of breath because parasites had attacked their respiratory systems, but she'd never been anyone's biological mother and never taken a child to raise except that child was already of school age and past most of the childhood diseases that were so common at that time and place.

My time on Pace's Branch may have been a serendipitous period of quarantine, because I was never sick while there, never contracted anything more serious than a cold. I did, however, pay a price for woefully inadequate dental hygiene.

In order to brush my teeth I'd take my brush and a glass of water and either some tooth powder or a mixture of salt and baking soda, and I'd go stand out by the fence across from the back porch wash stand. I brushed if I happened to think of it on my own, as I received no prompting from Bill or Mary, both of whom came closest to practicing dental hygiene when they picked their astonishingly-sound teeth with a broom straw. If we ran short of tooth powder, it might or might not go on the list for next month's trip to the Roxana store or up Kings Creek to Chet Mitchell's store.

There's no mystery then as to how I came to have four badly decayed molars, one in each side of both the upper and lower jaws, each one, absurdly enough for an eight-year-old, a permanent tooth. In the hollows of Letcher County a child's permanent tooth was permanent so long as it remained free of deep cavities and never ached so bad it had to be daubed with Oil of Cloves or "medicinal" whiskey. Then it was off to the dentist, a man whose main skill was tooth extraction. Saving a tooth more often meant, "Here, put this in your pocket, and try to keep your tongue out of the hole, haw-haw." I'd know my dental x-rays in the dark. For fifty years now I've seen the same picture of how my molars have migrated and tilted until I could floss them with baling twine.

I think now that I may have been predisposed to have soft tooth enamel and get cavities. That, in combination with unfluoridated well water, would seem to explain my early dental miseries. The sound yellow teeth of the Calihans must have been owing to the same good genes that protected them against so many other health threats to which they paid no heed.

Having bad teeth seemed to me at the time not such a bad thing, for, as the saying goes, it's an ill wind that blows no one good. My rotten teeth got me a rare ride in an automobile. And on the way to Whitesburg and the dentist, when Uncle Venon Whitaker's 1940 Chevy sedan left the graveled portion of the road and the noise inside grew suddenly quieter, I knew for the second time—the first being the school bus ride after the carbide-in-the-whiskey-bottle incident—what a wonder it was to glide along on a paved road. Oh, the speed. Forty-five miles per hour was to me the same as flying. That's what I remember of that day, the ride, and almost nothing at all of how a large stranger yanked four molars from my eight-year-old head.

There were other times when a medical professional might have eased my pain some and encouraged the healing process, but the people of Paces's Branch didn't run to the doctor for such trivial matters as an animal bite or a multitude of bee stings.

We knew, of course, that a bite from a "mad" dog could be fatal. Any dog that staggered around and shunned water had hydrophobia (rabies), so it was best to avoid such an animal, except to sneak up on it with a shotgun and shoot it dead at the first opportunity. The dog that bit me, on my hand and then again on the calf of my leg, was well known to us. He was a yellow cur of medium size that belonged to Lloyd Calihan just down the hollow from us. One day as we were on the way home after school, Jim and I were taking a shortcut through Lloyd's open barn when his dog slunk out of a stall door and attacked me. He didn't nip me; he bit hard, drawing blood from my hand and from my leg. Mary Calihan rubbed liniment on me to ease the soreness, but no one complained to Lloyd about his biting dog.

As for the bee stings, I had no one to blame but myself. If I'd thought to blame anyone at all, which I did not. It was a big adventure the time that Jim and I captured a swarm of bees and, following Bill's guidance, induced them to take up residence in one of his empty hives. A few stings, seven to be exact, didn't weigh much in the balance when a fellow was doing a manly job.

I'm sure Bill knew something about queen bees breaking off from their original colonies and taking a large portion of the worker bees along to light somewhere and become a separate colony. All Jim and I knew was that a cloud of bees had come flying up Pace's Branch and settled in one big wad on a low branch of a Peach tree. It was just our luck that the branch was an easy reach for two short specimens like us.

With no protective netting, no gloves, not so much as long-sleeved shirts, and without any smoke-making apparatus for calming the bees, we went at the limb with a handsaw. I'm not sure now of the details, but I think we just carried the severed limb, with the clump of bees attached, the short way from the peach tree to the empty hive and laid it in front of the hive and hoped for the best. The bees took to their new home and added to our supply of honey, so it was well worth a few stings, which weren't so terribly painful after Mary dabbed the welts with dampened baking soda.

Circa 1953: My mother, Chelsea Hogg, hangs laundry to dry on a clothes line in the back yard of our home on Halls Lane in Lexington, KY. She still washed clothes in the 1930s vintage Maytag wringer-type washing machine she'd used at our old house on Kings Creek in Letcher County. The machine now had an electric motor that replaced the original motor that ran on gasoline (or maybe it was kerosene) and needed a long flexible exhaust pipe to vent the fumes out of the house.

15   From Gettin' by to Gettin' Ahead

As I think of the grown-up men and women that I knew in my youth, I divide them into two groups as defined by how they sought to shelter, feed, and clothe themselves and their loved ones. There were those who were too defeated to entertain any pretensions about the future, and there were those who were simply too proud to yield to circumstances.

The gaunt people with thin lips and lined faces that city folks learned about in 1960s television documentaries were the defeated ones. They were the poor whites who, when the nation's social consciousness spiked, became to the outside world the "Face of Appalachia".

From birth these poor families were bound to the soil, and their children forewent formal education in order to begin early to help support the family. They began young and learned how to claw a living from digging in a coal mine, or plowing and hoeing a hillside cornfield, or wielding one end of a two-man crosscut saw in stands of second-growth timber. Marrying young, they went on to make large families of their own, more children to follow in the established pattern.

In the marginally more fortunate families, like the Hoggs and the Whitakers that I descended from, there was almost always a dominant no-nonsense father supported by a capable and compliant wife. Such a man had two requisite qualities for overcoming the circumstances he'd been born into: he was inordinately skilled at making a living by subsistence farming and he believed in the value of education as stoutly as he believed the Bible from cover to cover.

My dad, Hobson, and his brother, Isaac, managed against heavy odds to gain college educations. Tuition money was extremely tight, but they began teaching with "emergency" teacher certificates, and this allowed them to alternate between teaching the lower grades one term and attending college the next, and it meant they could pay their own tuition and other college expenses. As I've mentioned, my dad died in 1940, but my Uncle Isaac Hogg and many of my Whitaker aunts and uncles had their bachelor's degrees by the mid-1950s. That's when young baby boomers began to fill elementary school classrooms to the point of overflowing, which translated to an acute teacher shortage and opportunities for self-betterment in the teaching profession.

The war-time economic boom lasted years beyond war's end, but it was not the tide that lifted all boats. Lean times hung on in Letcher County. Many of her citizens left for the North, where their strong backs were worth more on the assembly lines than they were in the coal mines. The less well educated men and women left the mountains in droves to work in Detroit, Dayton, Youngstown, and other factory towns.

My aunts and uncles were predominantly educators, but they were poorly paid, and they too yearned for prosperity, for a standard of living that they knew they could never have on the salary of a Letcher County school teacher. The answer was obvious—leave the mountains.

Both branches of my extended family lived close to each other, geographically and socially, and no one wanted to leave the accommodating and hospitable village that was the extended family. But all saw the need to leave, and whether it was by a vote or by tacit agreement, the greater part of my father's generation of Hoggs and Whitakers left the hills.

If California's Salinas Valley was the Promised Land for the Joad family in Steinbeck's *Grapes of Wrath* as they fled Oklahoma and the Dust Bowl during the Great Depression, southern Indiana was the same, in a less desperate way, for most of my extended family.

There were many more Whitakers than Hoggs in this exodus. Granddaddy Jim Whitaker pulled up stakes as did thirteen of his children, at least ten of whom were adults at the time. For the Hoggs, there was my oldest living uncle, Chester Hogg, who had lead it all by moving several years earlier to Charlestown, Indiana to farm for a while and then live out his retirement years. Then in the 1950s Uncle Isaac Hogg moved his family to North Vernon, Indiana, and in just a few years he became superintendent of the county school system. The few non-teaching Hoggs and Whitakers and their spouses found work in various light industries in southern Indiana.

Some Letcher County people may be said to have "fled" eastern Kentucky beginning early in World War II. My kin that I'm telling about, the ones descended from my paternal grandmother, Larcena Hogg, and from my maternal grandfather, James Whitaker, didn't "flee" Letcher County, and they didn't join the war-time exodus, and they didn't leave *en masse*. They left in an orderly progression over a period of a few years in the early to mid nineteen-fifties. They settled in the small towns of southern Indiana in an area along I-65 that extends from just north of Louisville, in the south, to Columbus, Indiana, in the north. They spread over an area several times the size of Letcher County, Kentucky, but with the good Indiana roads the driving distances between their new homes were more as the crow flies and not a matter of skirting ten miles around a mountain ridge to reach a place just a mile away on a straight line. The families were effectively closer to each other than ever before and here they prospered as their dedication to their chosen profession was recognized and rewarded. Almost every one of them advanced through the ranks and retired as administrators or teacher-coaches.

It was well before President Lyndon B. Johnson's War on Poverty when both these large families, the Hoggs and the Whitakers, launched their own war against poverty. The Whitaker family's exodus probably wasn't an altogether singular event. Many other close-bound mountain families must surely have seen education, however hard it was to come by, as their pathway to opportunities beyond the hills.

My mother was the only one of that large family to venture forth from the hills with but an eighth grade education, and, not surprisingly, the only one of them for whom her working life would be a succession of cooking jobs.

Kick the can.

16 Under One Roof Again, Almost

In early 1949 Mother sent for me to come to Lexington and join her and three of my older siblings. Jim and I left Pace's Branch for good, me bound for Lexington and Jim going to live temporarily with an uncle at Whitesburg. We still wouldn't all be in the same place, but we were a little closer to that goal.

As I left Lower Kings Creek School in the middle of the fifth grade, I felt a little anxious at times about how I might be received by city kids. My defense mechanism was to imagine how a tough mountain lad would show those sissies in the city a thing or two. How wrong I was. I was shocked to learn just how tough city kids could be, and it remains one of the most memorable turnabouts in my thinking, that while life's hard knocks had made me thin-skinned and ready to take offence, I was not commensurately more fit for combat than were city kids.

Some of the kids of East Sixth Street were damned pugnacious, and I learned to be wary of the ones that growled and seemed all too ready to bite. At this late date I realize that my "toughness" then was just me acting out as a result of the pain and loss I'd seen at such a young age. I wasn't mean or tough; I was just carrying some anger I wasn't equipped to deal with. Perhaps my new Lexington classmates, those few who picked on me, were carrying similar baggage.

My oldest brother and my two oldest sisters had graduated high school and now worked bottom-tier jobs to help with the living expenses. We lived on Lexington's north side, about six blocks north of Main Street, in a two-storey brick building that had been cut up into four apartments. Our apartment was on the first floor. We had an indoor toilet, running water, a porcelain bathtub with claw feet, a gas range, and an ice box. The ice man came about once a week with a big block of ice. We put a big yellow card in the front window that announced to him how much ice we needed, 25, 50, 75, or 100 pounds, depending on which number was at the top of the card. All in all, our quarters were pretty plush. A bit crowded, but far better than any of us had experienced since leaving our home on Kings Creek.

Johnson Elementary School, some two blocks away on Sixth Street, was also a huge step up from the wooden school houses that accommodated eight grades in two rooms. Johnson was still fairly new, a handsome brick structure that the neighborhood could be proud of.

My fifth grade teacher was a dignified middle-aged lady who played the piano and led us in song at some point each day. I remember *Sweet Betsy from Pike*, a fine old tune for which there have accumulated enough rowdy lyrics in different parts of the country to make up dozens of earthy songs to say what Ike and Betsy did and what they endured. Our version was tame. Ike was her uncle and not her lover, and Betsy didn't get drunk, she didn't lose her virtue, and nobody was slaughtered as the wagons trekked across the prairie.

Our kindly teacher also read to us the young-adult version of Homer's *Odyssey*. An excellent story-teller, she kept us enthralled as the hero Ulysses faced one-eyed Cyclops and other monsters in his long journey back to Ithaca. Who could forget the wooden horse ruse? I found the tale as rousing as a cavalry charge in a matinee western.

Mother was pinching pennies in order to meet the rent payment, so I never ate lunch in the school cafeteria. I went home at noon, and the young lady whom I never regarded as a "baby sitter"—a city notion that I was unfamiliar with—gave me enough change to go the nearby Stinnett's Grocery and buy a can of Campbell's Tomato Soup and a ten-cent package of Hostess *Sno-Balls*. That and a homemade sandwich was my lunch every day during the school week. I never tired of the sameness; it was so superior to the old Kings Creek sameness of cold pork inside a cold biscuit.

For my winter wear in the city Mother bought me a new Mackinaw coat with a large flat collar that zipped up to become a hood. Wearing it gave me some confidence among my new schoolmates, and that lasted until one day when a little hoodlum bastard in a matching coat decided to torment me for having the gall to try and match his sartorial splendor. It still pisses me off to think of it, and all this time later I'd take pleasure in rapping his little cretin nose. I've never understood bullies. I say give them a pounding first, and then inquire into what it is about their unfortunate experience that causes them to victimize other children.

If my new milieu disabused me of the notion that I was tough, it also tested the view I'd tolerated in Roxana that it was okay to gawk and snigger at people just because they were bow-legged, or cross-eyed, or just weird. In our apartment building lived a young woman who was physically an adult, but she sometimes wore toy cap pistols in holsters and galloped along the sidewalk on her stick horse. My time in Roxana had acquainted me with persons needing but not always getting gentle loving care. It was good to see how devoted to this girl her older sister was.

Roxana had its coal miners, and our Lexington neighborhood had its farm laborers. Next door was a boarding house, and each morning a big red GMC panel truck with open sides and roll-up side curtains came from Calumet Farm, that storied home of Kentucky Derby winners, to pick up some workmen. The passengers in back sat on two long benches that faced each other. I learned many years later that horse farm laborers in 1950 were paid about five dollars a day. This was before light industry, and IBM in particular, came to Northeast New Circle Road in the mid-1950s to put pressure on the agrarian wage structure. Up until then a relative few of the landed gentry had held a preponderance of the local wealth and had managed to keep wages depressed.

As Halloween approached, I learned about "Trick or Treat". Halloween in Roxana had been about tricks, and treats were no part of it. The tricks amounted to wheel barrows in treetops, laundry on the line tied in knots, "rocking" the houses of selected victims, and egging cars, in the unlikely event that one dared pass by.

In my Lexington neighborhood the Halloween costumes for poor young boys, which included me and all my friends, were of two varieties: women's clothing or the ever-available rags of a hobo. Tricks were still played if goblins weren't properly appeased, but the tricks were of the milder sort. Soaping window screens was one of our tricks. "Tacking" window screens was another favorite, for the diabolical yet harmless fun it offered. We employed a long piece of twine, a safety pin, and a damp cloth. Tie the pin at one end of the twine and secure it to the center of the screen, then get behind a bush and pull the string taut and squeak the damp cloth along the twine and cause it to vibrate the screen and make an eerie sound.

If a utility pole had metal bars by which a lineman might climb it, we'd climb it, too, and hang lawn chairs at the top. I never participated in Halloween vandalism until we'd moved out to Halls Lane, a side street out Versailles Road near the western edge of town. There we sometimes set fire to the dry leaves in the storm drains so we could hide and watch as the smoke boiled out.

One memorable Halloween a kid had a BB gun, so we just naturally had to shoot out some light bulbs, especially the bulbs that were in a long string along the sidewalk in front of a place that sold used mobile homes. Someone called the cops that time and they arrived to shine their bright spotlight on Jim's back as he held the BB gun in front of himself and walked casually into Bill's Cafe, our little corner hangout that was just three doors from our house. Once inside, Jim stashed the BB gun behind the cigarette machine. We sweated it out, but the cops didn't bother to pursue the matter further. Perhaps there were worse kinds of vandalism happening in other parts of town and we were just small fish on a busy night for the law, but that was Halloween excitement.

Neither I nor any of my boyhood friends was ever arrested and taken to a juvenile detention facility, and I have to wonder why that was. Remembering what I was like as a kid, as I sloughed off my mother's words of guidance, as I stole a hubcap or two, and smoked and drank liquor in my mid-teens. I think my memory of that time has served to keep me humble as I assess the young people of today and think what might be the best way to combat antisocial behavior. I know I can never honestly support the idea of apprehension and incarceration as being the best way. I had a hard upbringing, but I had advantages that came to my rescue and kept me out of the clutches of the authorities. I was drawn to belong with a crowd of kids with chips on their shoulders, but my life was far from that of a kid in an intercity ghetto. Our saving grace was our naiveté. No one recruited us to peddle drugs, and all the adults in our lives sought to guide us along a path of obedience to the law, to our teachers, and to our elders.

In the neighborhood around Halls Lane in 1950 and 1951 I found some friends that I would keep through high school, and that was a new high water mark of stability in my life.

On summer evenings we played 'Kick the Can', setting the can in the center of the street and hiding behind houses, always hoping to be alone in the dark with a girl, and maybe getting to "first base" before "It" came along and discovered us and with a loud shriek raced us back to the can.

• • • • • • • •

I was happy, and well behaved too, for about three years. I received good marks at Picadome Elementary School, and the same was true for the seventh and eighth grades at Lafayette Junior High School. I joined the Boy Scouts, a troop that met up the street in the basement of Hillcrest Baptist Church. Perversely, this was not to be a character-building experience. It contributed to my early development, but not in an altogether propitious way. None of us could afford uniforms, and we never went on any trips where we would be expected to look like the scouts in *Boys' Life* Magazine. Our scoutmaster took a few of us once to Herrington Lake, about 35 miles south of Lexington, to a cabin he owned. There we raked leaves and cleared his yard of rocks. That night we slept in pup tents, and I shared a tent with two brothers who were both older than me. I lay jammed in between them, and they argued and fought most of the night. Next morning an irate farmer walked down through his field and into the shallow woods by the lake shore and wanted to know who the hell was in charge.

Scoutmaster Melvin F. asked the old man what his problem was. "What's my problem? I'll tell you my problem. My problem is that some eejit shot a gun into my pasture last night. Coulda killed one a' my cows." The .22 rifle lay beneath a sleeping bag in one of our tents, so we didn't protest the old man's claim. We took our upbraiding that included some quaint name-calling, like "dumb heads" and "half-raised hellions that belong in the reform school", and we apologized.

I suppose it was just our good luck that our next scoutmaster—Melvin had had enough of us after the trip to the lake—liked guns and was himself just a big kid. He took us to a real scout camp, Camp Offutt, on the Kentucky River in Woodford County. The only thing I recall of that trip was what we did after breakfast on the Sunday morning when we were preparing to break camp. Our new scoutmaster, Richard B., proudly showed us his Colt 45 Automatic pistol and allowed each of us to fire it out through the treetops toward the river. Fine, but we wanted to hit something more specific than the muddy river water, so we took turns propping our mess-kit spoons in the forks of a tree and seeing how near to the center we could place a bullet hole.

I was among my peers, in my comfort zone, hanging with a group of borderline miscreants none of whom required of me that I be anything other than what I was most comfortable with being. I needed those guys. I could have done worse in my choice of friends.

Circa 1950: The Hogg family home on Kings Creek by the mouth of Lucky Branch. This is the house where Stephen and Larcena Hogg raised their large family. "Granny Larce" passed in 1947, and this photo was taken after my Aunt Gladys and Uncle Isaac Hogg had come to live there with their young family. The photo shows a new coat of white paint. Evidence of modern conveniences inside the house is given by the electric service entering at the right side. For two summers in the early 1950s, when I was eleven and twelve years old, I came each summer from Lexington, KY to spend a joyous month with my aunt and uncle and my three double-first cousins.

Illustration by Jody

As official beer opener, I was bonding with my favorite uncle.

17 Keeping One Foot in the Hills

It's tricky for me to keep to a proper chronology of events during the three-year span that begins with my final departure from Pace's Branch when I went to live with my family in Lexington and ends when we'd been living for two years in our own home on Halls Lane on the western outskirts of Lexington.

All the adults, my mother, brother Manfred, and sisters Argyle and Erna, had jobs. Older brother Jim was still living with an uncle in Whitesburg. And I was too young to be left alone at home during the summer break from school. No one said to me that I was too young, but I know that's the reason they sent me back to Kings Creek during two successive summers to spend a month with Uncle Isaac and Aunt Gladys and their three children. Not that I minded, not at all. Being at their place on Kings Creek was like being at home, only better.

If I hold a benevolent view of my fellow man, I give weighty credit to the time I spent with my Uncle Isaac. And I thank my beloved Aunt Gladys for introducing me to a bill of fare that was a gastronome's delight and a huge step up from the country "grub" I'd so far subsisted on. I believe that they must have seen that despite my mother's efforts here was a child in need of some steady guidance and support. And all I felt at every turn was how good it was to be in the embrace of this family, there in the old homestead where Grandpa Stephen and Grandma Larcena had raised their large family.

In another of those brief but vivid old-time movies that lie close at hand in my bank of treasured memories, I can see Uncle Isaac's blue

1948 Chevy automobile sitting at the curb in front of our apartment on East Fourth Street, there, to my knowledge, for the express purpose of hauling me back to Kings Creek to spend a month or more in a place I loved.

Uncle Isaac, in his customary travelling garb of white shirt, gabardine slacks, and brown felt Fedora, with a Lucky Strike cigarette in the corner of his mouth, ducked inside just long enough to collect me and the brown paper sack that held my few items of clothing, a couple T-shirts, some underwear, two or three pairs of socks, and, without fail, one extra pair of bibbed overalls. A boy needed two sets of overalls, and no need at all for any more; one pair for wearing a week while the other pair made its way through the laundry cycle.

We headed east, cutting over to Third Street, which became Winchester Road, or U.S. 60, at the outskirts. Uncle Isaac was in no rush, especially after leaving U.S. 60 and the outer Bluegrass behind at Winchester and taking to State Route 15 that snaked along atop the knobs between the Bluegrass and the Cumberland foothills. I recall us stopping at a place called Pine Ridge, near Natural Bridge State Park, but I think we could have stopped some miles before that, because what ensued there led me to think we were in a "wet" county. Still, knowing how dry it has always been between Lexington and the Perry County (Hazard) line, I think now that there might have been a bootlegger on the premises.

The place was the prototypical country store, with more colorful and quaint advertising on the weathered board-and-batten exterior than any painter of nostalgic scenes would have the patience to consider. Lucky Strike, Chesterfield, Prince Albert, RC Cola, Carter's Little Pills, Lydia Pinkham's Tonic, Bing Crosby touting the mildness of Sir Walter Raleigh Pipe Tobacco, White Lily Flour, Brown's Mule plug chewing tobacco, cures for Piles, Stanback Headache Powders, and much more, including the easy-grab handle of the wooden-frame screen door, which like the screen door of every other country store, was branded with the name of a packaged and sliced bread (Light Bread) that was produced and packaged as far away as Knoxville, Tennessee.

Uncle Ike may have bought some smokes, and he most likely bought us some snacks. We were going to be on the road a good while inasmuch as a single mile of Highway 15 required as much time and careful driving as did any five miles of good road in places outside the hills. What I recall Uncle Ike bringing out to the car was a square little carton that said "Schlitz" on its side. He set it between us on the Chevy's wide bench seat, and once we got rolling again, he handed me a shiny new "church key" can opener and said to me, "Foyce (my family's pet name for me), rip the flap off that box and open me up a can of 'soup'." I suppose adults everywhere use euphemisms in the belief that they spare children from uncomfortable truths, but I was more than just comfortable with the situation; I swelled with pride at being Uncle Ike's right-hand man. I don't remember if we talked much, but it wouldn't have mattered, not when we were just cruising along with, as it seemed, not a care in the world. We'd get there when we got there, and I just hoped it wouldn't be too soon.

Uncle Ike didn't have an ice chest for the beer, and it was bound to get warm soon, so it mattered whether he chose to sip or he chose instead to let it slide on down a throat that in a dry county was too often parched and longing for the taste of a chilled beer. He gave his thirst a moderate quenching, and I was ever at the ready, never fumbling for the church key, endeavoring always to punch two evenly-spaced holes in the flat-topped cans and pass them from my left hand to his right hand with neither of us looking anywhere but at the road ahead.

Uncle Ike's intake slowed somewhat at about half-way through the six-pack, probably because the beer was warmer now, and foamy, and it sat heavier in his stomach. He rallied, though, when we got close to home and the clock was fast running down on our rolling Happy Hour.

"Foyce, Honey," he said, "maybe you can open me one more can of soup." I did. I hooked the edge of the opener on the lip of the can and, if I do say so, I expertly punched two very evenly-spaced holes through the top; no bartender could have done it better. And the warm beer spewed forth like a geyser, spraying me in the face and wetting the car's headliner. I was mortified, chagrined to my very marrow, to think I'd slammed the lid on the most agreeable time I'd ever experienced in the company of an adult. I glanced cautiously up at Uncle Ike; he was smiling. Beer dripped from my eyebrows, and Uncle Ike was chuckling, so softly at first that I could only discern it by his quivering belly. And then he busted out laughing.

We didn't have a towel, no paper napkin, nothing. Maybe I could have unbuckled my overall galluses and pulled my T-shirt off and used it to blot the beer from the headliner, but we let it slide. So there the stain remained, for as long as Uncle Ike owned that car, as a lasting indictment of our unspoken complicity to suck all the pleasure to be had from one memorable summer day.

It was a vacation for me, that month with Uncle Isaac and Aunt Gladys and their three children all of whom were my double-first cousins. Wade was about my age, and he had a little brother and a little sister.

Rural Electrification had just recently come to Kings Creek and Aunt Gladys had a new Kelvinator refrigerator in Granny's old kitchen. That was great for me, because Aunt Gladys could make my favorite dessert any time she chose to. She'd layer banana slices in a bowl of Strawberry Jello, and after it set she'd skim the cream off a fresh bucket of milk and with her electric egg beater she'd beat it into a stiff mound of sweet whipped cream. She knew I was crazy for the stuff, and it pleased her to see her "men" take such delight in the treats she plied us with. It was our extreme good fortune that Aunt Gladys was, like her husband, a school teacher and could spend her summers spoiling us.

She found chores for me and Wade, and the two of us strove to find ways to have some fun with whatever task she set us to do. (If anyone reading this is a member of PETA, I beg you to forgive what two eleven-year-old boys did when they were charged with rounding up the free-range poultry that were destined for Aunt Gladys's big deep freezer.)

One morning, after the breakfast dishes were cleared off the big table, Aunt Gladys said to us, "Boys, today we're gonna put some frying chickens in that new freezer. So get out there and round me up about two dozen pullets. Just wring their necks and leave 'em by the big kettle. Then fill it with water from the well and build me a good fire under it so we can scald 'em and pluck 'em."

We had our orders, and except for the bit about wringing their necks, we couldn't see much in the way of fine print that stood in the way of our making it a challenge to our inventiveness. And "wring their necks", said as it was in such an off-hand way, seemed to us open to interpretation, so we interpreted it as "kill 'em".

Well, you can't kill 'em until you catch 'em, and a chicken will run just fast enough to stay a few inches ahead of the end of your arm. We made a couple of fruitless chases and then took a break to consider by what means we might extend our natural reach. A rubber garden hose happened to be lying at the base of Granny's big apple tree out back of the smoke house. What good was a garden hose on a place where the only running water was in the creek across the road? None that we could see. So we took out our pocket knives and each cut off about a foot of hose. We hefted the things, took a few practice swings, and together exclaimed, "Blackjacks".

The only blackjacks we were familiar with—we had seen them on occasion in Roxana as they were flaunted by various of our village ruffians—consisted of a banana-sized basket-weave leather pouch that was filled with lead shot and attached to a handle that might or might not have a spring inside it to give it that little extra bit of "whip" so that it didn't take a vicious roundhouse swing, but rather a love-tappish sort of stroke, to lay a man out cold. And, generally, the blackjacks were in fact black, and they had a black leather wrist strap. Ours would be the faded green of a rubber garden hose that had been left in the sun for a long time.

We "loaded" our country blackjacks by whittling three-inch wood stoppers and driving them into the business end of the hose pieces. We finished them off by boring holes at the opposite ends through which we looped some baling twine to serve as wrist straps, and we were ready to resume the poultry roundup.

Without going into unnecessary detail, I'll just say that we employed our blackjacks to anesthetize the chickens, and only then did we wring their necks. They died peacefully, and not one of them ran around "like a chicken with its head cut off", which satisfied my cousin and me that we'd done the humane thing for them.

During our years of living with the Calihans on Pace's Branch, Jim and I had made brief visits to the home of Aunt Gladys and Uncle Isaac, usually just overnight stays that didn't allow us enough free time to invent activities that might get us into trouble. But this time Cousin Wade and I faced a month of freedom, and we had a blank agenda; no Vacation Bible School, no visits to libraries, no mental or spiritual tedium, just a few daily chores that we did willingly and with all dispatch. And then we were free to go to any part of the fields or the woods, or to the creek, and free to do about anything within our limited means, just so long as we didn't take foolish risks or aggravate a neighbor.

We never caught a fish—the summertime flow of Kings Creek was slow, shallow, and much too clear for that—but it wasn't about catching, it was about the anticipation, doing all the things we thought would enable us to catch a fish, the pursuit. Taking "game" on dry land, however, was, at least to our uninformed way of thinking, a successful undertaking. We had guns, and we could see our quarry. And if it bore fur, feather, or even scales, it was our quarry; mammals, birds, reptiles, and amphibians.

We were country kids who'd not yet learned that there were ecosystems and that we'd all be better off if we appreciated the interdependence of species. Our older relatives might be said to have had dominion over all non-human life forms, as was God-given in the Old Testament. They had few qualms about killing wildlife. Wade and I, on the other hand, didn't proceed from any conscious belief or understanding, and certainly not from any sense of Divine Permission; we'd learned by example about killing things, and then we made some childish assumptions about what was fair game.

As for qualms about killing wildlife, permit me an aside here to tell of an undertaking by some cousins of mine in which a wild creature was well in hand, was experimented with, and then permitted to go its way, as best it could. These cousins were about as wild as anything else that lived near them at the head of their hollow. One warm spring day they happened upon a rattlesnake that had come down from its den up on the ridge. The snake had chosen the footpath as a place to sun itself, so the boys saw it from a distance. While one of the pair was fashioning a long forked stick with his pocket knife, the other ran home and returned with one of his momma's old silk stockings. Since the rattler wasn't coiled for striking, they approached it as quietly as they could and pinned its head to the ground with the pronged stick. Then with a Popsicle stick they pried opens the snake's mouth, and with not much urging, the snake sank its fangs into the stocking that was dragged past it. One good yank and out came the fangs, whereupon they lifted the prong from the snake's neck and allowed it to wriggle away. And the boys had a souvenir that would guarantee an audience any time they chose to tell of their little adventure.

If venomous snakes can regrow fangs, as I'm told by various websites they can, and if this particular rattler had recently killed and eaten, say, a fair-sized rodent, then he probably wouldn't starve before he was equipped with new fangs and could once again kill his prey. Not that two country boys would give a crap if a poisonous snake never ate again—they likely said, "Alright, you sonofabitch, if you get hungry, you just go and gum sumpin' to death, if you can."

Uncle Isaac never told me and Cousin Wade what to kill and what not to kill. Before permitting us to go out shooting, though, he instructed us on the safe handling of two .22 rifles, a Stevens semi-automatic with a scope, and the bolt-action single-shot Remington Model 41 that had belonged to my late father. The old single-shot required that you pull back the bolt, drop a single bullet into the chamber, close the bolt, and then pull back the bolt head to cock it. You had one chance to take a fine bead and hit your target, and if you missed the bird, squirrel, or rabbit, it would be in the next county before you were prepared to shoot again. It was the better rifle for learning marksmanship, and at eleven years of age I had no nervous tics, no aches or pains, no weaknesses or afflictions to throw off my aim. I knew nothing about ballistics, about windage or elevation; I just was able to draw a fine bead and hold it steady. The little single-shot "plinker" did the rest. It shot true. If I lined the front and rear sights up on the head of a water snake out in the shallow creek, it was as good as dead. True, these were harmless creatures, but in the country, a snake was a snake, and one of them had, after all, bitten me when I was a toddler, and even though my maternal granddaddy later taught me that a blacksnake in a corn crib was a good thing, because it killed and ate the rats that otherwise pillaged the corn, for that one summer I was a callous killer, of snakes at least.

One can argue that a .22 rifle was too much power in the hands of an eleven-year-old, but I bless Uncle Isaac for allowing me that heady experience. Handling a .22 rifle was much less of a threat to my health and well being than a lot of other activities that I undertook on my own, unarmed and unsupervised.

Uncle Isaac didn't own a mule or a horse, no draft animal of any kind, yet he still managed to grow a corn crop and some soy beans. Around 1947, he took the unusual step for a mountain farmer of buying an International-Harvester Farmall Cub tractor, complete with plows, disc harrow, sickle bar mower, and a steel utility wagon. Cousin Wade could handle the tractor, and that summer he and I went on errands with the tractor, to plow an occasional field or to take the wagon and haul feed and supplies from Roxana. The little tractor may have had a "road" gear, I don't know, but we always crept along the gravel road at a comfortable plowing speed, with Wade in the bouncy driver's seat and me standing on the draw-bar or at times stepping off to walk alongside.

On one of our trips to Roxana we encountered a girl we knew from school and who was about our age, and we ended up regretting that encounter. I don't remember the girl's real name, her classmates all just called her "Nehi", not because she stood any shorter than most girls of her age, but because she was so extremely fond of the soft drink by that name. She might have escaped the nickname had she not also been so willing at recess to give clogging exhibitions in which she did some truly remarkable footwork. She had talent, but her willingness to show it to her ignorant classmates just made her all the more vulnerable to teasing.

It shames me to say it, but on the road that day we teased that poor girl in a most unbecoming way. But to Nehi's everlasting credit, she kept some dignity about her and didn't pursue our sniggering enjoinders. She may have cussed us—I hope she did, as we deserved it—but she wouldn't be baited into the colorful tirade we'd hoped for.

Nehi went her way on up the creek in the direction we'd come from, and we went ours. We stopped at the store in Roxana and got whatever Uncle Isaac had sent us to get, and then we began our interminably slow way back up Kings Creek's gravel "highway".

Uncle Isaac met us at the front gate, heading us off before we could drive to the barn and unload the wagon. Oh, Hell, Nehi had been there; she'd told Uncle Isaac the whole sordid story. We were in trouble, and I could tell that we had more than just an ordinary scolding coming. "Boys," Uncle Ike said, and I was too scared to remember what else he said. From the tone of his voice I could sense his deep displeasure and knew that a serious talk, or worse, was coming.

We pled guilty with mitigating circumstances, which is to say that we cast some blame on poor blameless Nehi and in that maneuver dodged a thrashing. I was afterward dogged by guilt and wishing that I had just made a full confession and got it over with. Uncle Ike spared the rod, and I wallowed in guilt. My uncle, the last of my father's many siblings, died in 1995, and I regret that I never thought to confess my wrongdoing while the opportunity was available to me. If I had told my good and kind uncle that he was one person in my life that I had never wanted to disappoint, perhaps he would have known how dear he was to me.

18 I Like Ike

At school in Lexington in November of 1952 I have the easy task of being General Dwight D. Eisenhower's campaign manager in our seventh grade homeroom mock presidential election. It's almost too easy, because Ike is a hero with a tide of approbation pushing him toward the Whitehouse. We walk all over Adlai Stevenson and my pretty opposite number, Patty M. I've got a crush on Adlai's campaign manager, so I don't crow over an easy victory.

Senator Joe McCarthy is all over the TV, insisting that our state department is a nest of communists and communist sympathizers. Rock n' Roll hasn't happened yet, and Elvis Presley is still at home in Tupelo, Mississippi, driving a truck and three years away from the Sun Recording Sessions in Memphis that will launch his career.

Meanwhile, I'm getting to know my mother. We work together in the evenings at a restaurant in downtown Lexington, and our kitchen complicity bonds us even as it provides a bit of recreation. I see the nervous boss and his big-bosomed, diamond-sparkly wife through the eyes of this impish mother I hadn't known before. Who knew she had a borderline-wicked sense of humor and loved to laugh?

My job is to wash dishes, but I steal opportunities to do a little experimental cooking for myself, and I learn that with egg batter and cracker crumbs one can deep fry anything that passes for organic matter. We take the bus home after closing up at 11:00 PM. The late nights don't seem to affect my scholastic performance in the eighth grade.

Our house on Halls Lane is next door to a place that makes concrete burial vaults, and the sprawling lot filled with rejected vaults is a fine place for me to hang with my buddies, swapping jokes that are clumsily graphic and sneaking smokes. I disappoint my pals by loving the Brooklyn Dodgers and mostly ignoring the Cincinnati Reds.

I'm not dating yet, so I'm not overly self-conscious about my limited wardrobe. On Mondays at school, I'm glad I've earned a few bucks and can go through the hot line in the cafeteria and have an entree and two sides, like franks and beans with sauerkraut or mashed potatoes. Hot, wholesome, and filling.

We're two years from owning a TV, but I feel I know quite a bit about Sgt. Joe Friday of *Dragnet* because a dufus classmate is keeping everyone well posted on that important matter, always going "dum da dum dum" and "the facts, ma'am, just the facts", causing our teacher to roll his eyes. Mr. D is in cahoots with the rest of us, as much entertained as we are by our lovable bumpkin.

At home, at work, at school, or lying low with my pack of miscreant friends, I'm going with the flow. Not comparing different times, not setting myself up with expectations. It's the 1950s, and although I have no sense of living in a favored time—which I'm told it was, at least for white suburban families—I'm happy to get out of bed each day and see what's happening.

19   Young Sharecropper

When we first moved out to the west side of Lexington, I was in the sixth grade and still too young to get a work permit, but that didn't mean I was too young to work. I worked that summer, not for wages, but for a share of the vegetables I would grow in the garden of a household further west out Versailles Road. I don't recall how we came to know the Atkins family, but their pretty white frame house sat on a plot large enough to accommodate a rose garden, a vegetable garden, and several mature fruit trees out back. I don't know why they trusted a young boy to tend their plot and pick their cherries. I must have told them a good story touting my experience with growing vegetables at the Calihan's. The Atkinses would be pleased to share their produce with me, and later in the summer I was proud to take my share of the green beans, potatoes, and corn home to my mother.

I was actually paid in cash for picking the cherries, five dollars. I stood on a ladder picking those luscious cherries, and my thin upper body was sweat-streaked and smudged with the black powdery residue from the branches of the cherry tree. I took the five-dollar bill home and stashed it in a Kodak Brownie camera, the camera I had gotten for a birthday, the camera with which I shot one roll of film which was never to be developed because I couldn't see laying out my hard-earned cash to see what I'd already seen and could see again whenever I wanted to. I must have soon earned a little more money, for how else would I have forgotten that five dollars for a whole year?

It was the following summer when one day I noticed the camera and idly thought to open the back. And, miracle of miracles, I went from being penniless to making plans for how to blow five dollars. Castlewood Swimming Pool, on the far side of Lexington, was open. It meant a bus ride downtown, a transfer to the Loudon Avenue bus and another bus ride to the extreme northern edge of the city. But I had the coin for it all, the bus fare, admission to the pool, rental fee for a pair of ill-fitting swim trunks that had been worn by any number of poor kids before me. Plus, I could spring for a chili dog and a root beer at the ramshackle restaurant that sat across from Castlewood Park.

The Atkinses were a dignified couple sharing a house with an elderly man who was the father of the man of the house. They were kind to me while at the same time allowing me to maintain a semblance of dignity. The old man was tall and lean, and as he went about applying bone meal to his roses he wore a collarless shirt and a flat straw boater; he resembled pictures I'd seen of old-time Philadelphia Athletics Manager Connie Mack. After he died, Mrs. Atkins gave me some of his clothes, of which I remember only the socks, thin and silky, the kind that required a sock garter to keep them up out of one's shoe tops. But they were without holes, so I wore them. For a while there I didn't have to mend holes in my old socks with adhesive tape and then ink the tape so it wouldn't draw attention to my Achilles tendon. Those silky socks felt pretty good on my feet, and I'm still grateful. And I feel lifted just now, recalling a kindness that a gentle soul did for me.

20   Before Astroturf or Sports Medicine

My summer activities following both seventh and eighth grade were about evenly divided between time spent trying to earn money and time devoted to doing nothing with my friends. It wasn't nothing, exactly; it was just that we did nothing that cost money. Our parents had little discretion about how their money was spent. Their spending priorities were fixed. After paying the mortgage, the utilities, and the grocery bill, if anything was left over, we kids weren't so naïve as to think it would go toward anything as truly extravagant as, say, a baseball glove. Most parents on Halls Lane had themselves lived through the Great Depression, and while they wanted better lives for their children, they'd be damned if they'd pay actual cash money to save an idle child from summer boredom. "You're bored? Well, let's by all means see that you are not bored. Go mow the damn grass. Try your hand at doing the laundry. Or try standing all day in one spot on an assembly line. Then talk to me about bored."

In that way our parents motivated us to find our own fun. And we did. We lacked the means to tune out the world; we had no iPods, no cell phones, no video games, and no personal computers. To be inside on a sunny day was the same as being in a prison; almost all the fun to be had was outside, and mostly right in the middle of our dead-end street.

We kids had each other, and we engaged fully with each other, and we created unforgettable fun, all on our own. Kick-the-Can, Capture the Flag, Fox and Hounds, War, Cowboys and Indians. And team sports, too, especially baseball and football. If we had a baseball, one single baseball, with or without a cover, or if one of us had a football, we were in business. And we didn't need adults to tell us how. We didn't need a referee to adjudicate our disputes. If it took a fight, then that's what it took. We may have learned some things that we'd later benefit by unlearning, but we also grew individually more self-reliant, and we did it more quickly and thoroughly, I think, than happens for kids in today's organized youth sports.

Of course I envied the three or four lucky boys whose dad's bought them baseball gloves and spikes and drove them to Little League practices and games. Still those others of us for whom Little League didn't even exist, we made do. We chose sides and played ball in the long lot that lay between the back yards on the east side of Halls Lane and the Huber & Huber Truck Terminal. We didn't have ground rules, so if a long fly ball fell between the parked trailers it was still in play, and a sure home run, even for a couple of woefully slow blubber-butts in our group.

Our brand of baseball was in theory a non-contact game, but we operated under a paucity of rules. There was ready agreement on three strikes, three outs, and nine innings; everything else was adjudicated case-by-case. Close calls were contested but usually resolved quickly, except when there was contact between a base runner and a fielder covering a bag, or when a base runner was deemed to have run out of the imaginary base path to avoid a tag. Since we lacked the means of marking off the base paths, their invisible boundaries shifted according to the conflicting needs of the runner and the fielder. Tags were apt to become outright slugs that ignited shoving matches, grappling in the dust, kicking and biting, and much loud swearing.

As for football, we hadn't heard of flag football, in which grabbing a flag from a ball carrier's hip pocket was judged the same as a tackle, and we seldom deigned to play "touch" football. With no helmets, no cleats, and no pads, we played the tackle version of football. But hard hits and head-on collisions were rare, since the defender was almost always trying for a take-down from behind. Still, though, about once in every game someone got in a good hit. With his feet planted, the defender would crouch low as the ball carrier came on as though to run him over, and there the accident would happen. A bony shoulder would smash into a soft solar plexus, and the ball would go flying and precipitate a mad free-for-all for its possession. While on the ground and for the moment ignored, the ball carrier rolled side to side clutching his abdomen and trying to get air back into his lungs.

Once in each game, that's the most often it happened. Someone got hurt. It didn't matter that it was a clean lick or that we knew the risks we took by playing tackle football without protective padding. The player on the ground rained curses upon his opponent, and if he couldn't hold back the tears, he'd cuss all the louder. And that would be it for football, until the next time.

Illustration by Jody

Oh no! What have I done?

21   Fledgling Entrepreneur

The following spring as I neared the end of the eighth grade and as lawns were greening and filling with dandelions, I scouted around our neighborhood for lawns that I could mow. This took me to the older and more expensive homes up on Versailles Road, as no one on Halls Lane would pay someone to mow their grass. Except for one or two elderly ladies on our street, the neighbors, most all of them blue collar workers, did their own home maintenance chores. If something broke, they fixed it themselves.

Out along U.S. Route 60, which we in west Lexington called Versailles Road, the residents were old timers living in homes that I don't doubt were paid for in full, and even I could see they were a class above those of us living on the side streets. Luckily for me, these nicer homes had their own lawn mowers; the mostly older residents just needed a kid like me to push their mower around their weedy lawns. I was thrilled to receive a dollar for two or three hours of pushing a gasoline-powered mower that lacked the most basic of safety features that home owners of today take for granted. The typical mower lacked a full shroud, and viewed from the front or back one could see the spinning blade. Any stick or rock was apt to become a projectile that menaced anyone in the vicinity. Thrown rocks were a constant danger to the ankles of the kid behind the thing.

Older brother Manfred surprised me with his generosity that summer by springing for a brand new mower. It was a shiny dark green model from Montgomery Ward, and I recall it was powered by a

Lauson engine. I was proud to push that pretty machine along the sidewalks from one mowing job to the next. Part of the deal was that I had to mow our own grass at home, and also mow the yard where Manfred and his new bride lived on Cisco Road, and that was more than fair.

In my enthusiasm for mowing grass and making money I was loath to turn down a job, and that led me to one job that ended up being a dreadful abuse of my shiny new machine. Bill's Café sat on the corner of Halls Lane and Versailles Road, a little more than a hundred yards from our house, and I spent much of my free time there. Bill was a kindly man and much loved by his cooks and waitresses and the regulars who came for the superb chili and bean soup, and the burgers—one dollar for a sack of five burgers to go.

I liked the big Wurlitzer juke box that would spin a forty-five RPM record for just a nickel, and Bill always kept two pinball machines, and these too cost just a nickel a game. If you racked up a good score, you could win free games. And if you could cause the silver ball to roll more slowly, you could manipulate it to hit more bumpers more often. This was cheating of course, and risking a scolding by Bill, who was so good-natured that a scolding from him lay on ones conscience longer than if he'd been the sort to just cuss us out real good.

Inside Bill's place is where my pals and I waited for the school bus to take us to Lafayette Junior High School on the south side of Lexington. We got to Bill's each morning with about fifteen minutes to spare, time for a few games of pinball. Bill would be at the griddle busily filling breakfast orders for hot cakes, fried eggs and sausage, or ham, or bacon, and coffee. As he concentrated on the busy griddle, Bill's back was to us, and we could stealthily lift the pinball machine and place the front two legs on top of the player's toes. This quite literally "leveled the playing field" by slowing the travel of the ball so the player could make it slam repeatedly off a bumper with loud clangs as the score mounted up by increments of 1,000 points or more, depending on whether the bumper was temporarily lit up. Of course, if the player got too rough, whacking the flippers and hunching his hips against the machine, it would "tilt" and punish the player by cancelling the game and eating his nickel.

I have so many happy memories from Bill's Café. I'd have done just about anything for Bill, and when he asked if I'd mow the back yard at his new home on Mason-Headley Road, I didn't hesitate to say "yes". The following Saturday morning I pushed the still-new mower up the sidewalk to the café where Bill loaded it in the back of his new 1955 blue and white Chevy station wagon.

Bill was a good man; that I've never doubted; it was just that he knew no more about machinery than I did. Else he would never have lured me and my mower to that overgrown lot. Horseweeds, rag weeds, milkweeds with stalks almost an inch in diameter and head tall, plantain and dock, and just about every other noxious weed imaginable waved over that quarter-acre that he called a back yard. The builder had scraped it off months before with a bulldozer, and since then it had grown apace. But those weeds didn't impress me. I had the answer, didn't I? I had a gas-powered mower of at least three horsepower, the power of three horses. Just imagine.

The trusty Lauson engine started with a single pull of the starter rope. I shoved it into the mass of foliage, for about three feet, where it coughed and quit. After much trial and error, I was about to become discouraged, but I brightened when I accepted that there was only one way to attack this mess. I couldn't simply push the mower deck against the stalky weeds. I'd have to press down on the mower handle and tilt the blade back forty-five degrees and allow it to gnaw sideways through the fibrous weed stalks. It took me hours, tilting and pushing ahead for a foot or so and then backing up, bringing the blade level, and making a finishing pass.

I got the job done, and I was paid what we'd agreed on, or, knowing Bill, he may have added a little extra for all the trouble it had been. But whatever the amount, it didn't begin to cover the damage I'd unknowingly done to my fine new mower. All the damage wasn't done that day, but the mower had taken a beating and the stage was set for the catastrophe that followed.

The next time I added gas to the tank, which was integral with the engine cowling, it leaked out onto the mower deck. Of course this had to have been due to the rough treatment I gave the mower in Bill's back yard. Regardless, I couldn't mow any more yards and I couldn't earn any more money until the problem was fixed. The question was how do you fix a leaky gas tank? The handiest solution was quick and cheap; buy an add-on tank, mount it low on the handle, and run a rubber gas line from the new tank to the carburetor.

Brother Manfred bought the little fuel tank, about one quart capacity, and I mounted it on the mower handle with baling wire and ran a rubber tube between it and the carburetor. I mowed a couple of yards, and all seemed fine, no leaks, no problems. Then it was time to mow the yard at the place that Manfred had rented as the first home for him and his recently-wed wife. I started it up and mowed for a while, and then I killed the engine while I moved some garbage cans out of the way. I went to wrap the starter rope around the pulley, and in the process I knocked the fuel line loose, which was just waiting to happen since I hadn't known to clamp the ends onto the fuel exit and entry points. They had gone on snug, so what would have been the point?

For a few seconds the fuel poured onto the hot muffler which of course vaporized it, which, as I was to learn, is essential for gasoline to combust. With no clue of the impending disaster, I wasted no time in pushing the loose tube back onto the carburetor inlet. Nor, unfortunately, did I waste time in winding the starter rope on the pulley and giving it a firm yank.

Hindsight tells me two things. *One*: gasoline vapors are heavier than air, meaning that the vapors sank to the mower deck and lingered there over a small puddle of gasoline; and *Two*: unlike modern mowers which have a rubber boot covering the point where the plug wire connects to the sparkplug itself, the connection on my mower was just bare-ass naked, metal-to-metal, and subject to giving off a teeny, tiny, scarcely-visible spark when the engine was cranked.

I tugged hard on the starter rope, and the engine obeyed by firing right up, as did the lingering gas fumes. I leapt back and swore an oath as flames erupted around the engine. A metal fuel line might have saved the day, but my jerry-rigged rubber tube fried and melted away, and a steady little stream of gasoline fed the fire. I couldn't think how to put it out, and as I stood, mute and horrified, the flames rose and billowed and turned my shiny green machine into a hideous smoking black heap of useless metal.

I don't recall if I ever thanked my big brother properly for not killing me, so I'll do it now. Thanks, Big Brother.

22 The Supporting Cast

It's pleasurable to recall how I spent my later childhood years, who my friends were and what we did together, but it requires some effort to bring other family members into my picture of back then. It was a "me" time. On Halls Lane in the early 1950s our whole family, almost, was together under one roof, as my mother had vowed we would be. Jim was still living with one of our mother's brothers in Whitesburg. At least, though, he was with close family, and so we had the feeling, after being scattered apart for so long, of all being together. But just as importantly for me at the time, I was among my peers every day, and not just at school. For the first time since earliest childhood I had friends within hollering distance, just down the street. I belonged to a social group other than the one that fed and sheltered me.

From that point on, up until I married and left home, I contrived to be self-regulated. That didn't mean much since I didn't have any money to spend, and if you're dead broke you're not as likely to get into any serious trouble. Still, I had a kind of freedom, and I disdained to have it impinged upon by practical or moral guidance from my mother or my older siblings.

We'd each one of us made the best of disparate tough situations, but I believe that my mother and I bore the most emotional scars; she and I had been the least equipped to endure the years of family separation. In our home on Halls Lane she and I were together again, and I still respected and trusted my mother. We shared the practical aspects of a mother-son interdependence, but our connection must have suffered some damage in our years apart. At eleven, twelve, and thirteen years of age I saw my mother as hopelessly old-fashioned and out of touch, and I didn't ask her for much advice. When she did counsel me, I listened, but I absorbed little.

In the meantime, my oldest two siblings progressed from being underemployed to having better jobs, and soon they found more fitting employment at the General Electric Lamp Plant on Rosemont Gardens, where the product was sealed-beam headlamps for automobiles. Manfred, an incipient engineer, excelled at tool and die making and made the best of his time with GE. Sister Argyle worked on the assembly line. Irene, the middle child, got married in her late teens, so she wasn't much of a presence in our house at the time.

Argie was a sweet big sister and good to me and Jim. As Jim and I grew into our teens, she, more than our mother, demonstrated a sense of the day-to-day practical needs of her younger brothers. Sometimes when she'd gotten her pay from GE she'd go to the trouble of finding and bringing home exactly the clothing item one of us needed, usually a shirt or trousers. It was always a happy surprise to have something new to wear to school or on a date.

· · · · · · · ·

Earlier, In December of 1948 while Jim and I still lived with the Calihans, Mother had sent word in a letter that Jim and I had a new baby sister and that her name was Dana. But Dana wasn't really her name—that's just what my mother's hand writing looked like to Bill Calihan, and he was the one reading the letter aloud to me and Jim. It was several months later that we learned that our baby sister's real name was Donna.

Donna's father was Mother's longtime love interest, Bob Caudill. I have long wished for them that they could have made a happy couple, sharing and caring for each other, but that wasn't to be, and Mother's time with Bob in Lexington was, to my knowledge, the last serious romantic relationship she would enter into.

It was a few months after learning of our new little sister that Jim and I got to meet her, and that was when we came to Lexington for a summer visit. Donna was a cute little toddler who was to grow to become an altogether winsome young lady. I was about twelve when I began to help look after her. My older siblings worked day shifts while Mother stayed home with Donna and I was at Lafayette Junior High

School. Then in the evening, Mother would catch the bus to the downtown restaurant where she stood on her feet and cooked for eight hours at a stretch. It fell mostly to me and big sis Argyle, whom we all called "Argie", to keep an eye on "Doodie", which was Argie's name for Donna because Argie thought her to be as adorable as a doodie, a word in our old mountain parlance for a fuzzy baby chick.

We had a gray and white cat named Boots who birthed a litter of kittens in our basement. No one suspected that Donna was mobile enough to slide her bottom one step at a time and get down the wooden cellar steps on her own to check out the kittens. We learned of her newfound facility and her daring only after she'd found the tiny kittens, with their eyes still closed, and accidentally tumbled some heavy crates onto their bed. We heard the pitiful mewing and I was sent to see what was the matter. Donna was a baby herself, so it was doubly sad for me to look upon the tragic scene. The kittens were maimed, and Donna was both bereft and perplexed. And I was a tearful mess. What to do first, comfort my baby sister or attend to the suffering kittens?

I scooped Donna up and took her upstairs to Mother, and then it was my job to do the merciful thing for the kittens. Which I did, over in the lot next door where the concrete burial vault plant dumped their rubble. With speed being of the essence, and with tears streaming down my face, and lacking any decent means of euthanizing the kittens, my method was crude, but in my heart it was not callous, and I know I did the best that could be expected from a twelve-year-old. Little Donna was blameless, as I believe I was too.

I soon forgot about the incident, but it may have weighed in my decision years later to put away my shotgun and never again kill a bird or mammal, and to remember and regret the times that I had done so. I remember the hunts, the camaraderie, and how I exulted in achieving a bag limit of squirrels, or rabbits, or doves. The change came during a dove shoot, when I winged a bird, not damaging it enough to kill it outright, just enough to ensure it would never fly again, the kind of shot I kicked myself for. The bird glided to earth between corn rows, and I went to retrieve it. It walked toward me as though unafraid. Why was it not trying to take flight and escape? Clearly, it was addled, would never fly again, and if I left it there it would be easy prey for a fox. What cinched it for me, the thing that quenched forever my already-faltering willingness to kill things, was a single drop of blood seeping from one eye of the bird and clinging there, accusing more compellingly than words ever could. There was nothing for it but to snap its delicate neck, and as I did so I remembered the kittens.

· · · · · · · ·

Halls Lane was two miles from the busy intersection of Main and Limestone Streets, and close to downtown as the crow flies, but it was considered to be "out in the county". The street was one very long block that dead-ended at a cornfield beyond which were railroad tracks, and beyond the tracks was a great limestone cavity that had been blasted and chiseled out of the earth by The Central Rock Company. For me, the best thing about that big hole is that it contained a lake that covered two or three acres. In quarrying deep for the limestone, the company had struck one of the many underground streams that course among the layers of limestone that underlie the central Bluegrass and are the source of the "limestone water" that has long been credited with giving a nutritional edge to Kentucky-bred horses.

I didn't know all that back then, but I knew that fish lived in water, and I was bound to see if any lived in this place that I soon regarded as my private fishing hole. I was fourteen in 1953 when brother Manfred was inducted into the U.S. Army and sent to Fort Devens, Massachusetts for training and then on to Germany where his leadership abilities played well in his role as a drill instructor. He was still single and living at home at the time of his induction, and at home is where he left all his fishing gear. I made good use of it, or bad use, as I think he would have called it. I hadn't yet learned to tie the "Improved Clinch" knot to attach an artificial lure to the line, so I used the one knot that's sneered at by just about every fisherman, sailor, or boy scout: that worthless, stinking, damn "granny" knot. I think I emptied his tackle box all in one spring, flung every last poorly-secured lure far out into the lake. I was soon reduced to using a cane pole and digging worms for bait, but that comedown worked for me, as I began to catch some small bream and catfish along the rocky shore line.

One summer day I had the quarry to myself and was "drowning worms" and idling the hours away when an older boy showed up, a biggish lout whom I knew as an upper-classman at Lafayette High, a fellow who didn't strike me as completely trustworthy. We chatted for a bit, with me all the while trying and failing to care about anything that was on his mind. After talking his way up to it, he pulled from his pants pocket a .22 caliber Derringer pistol and fired a few rounds into the water. I wasn't picking up on anything to make me truly fear for my wellbeing. After all, if I'd been lucky enough to own a .22 pistol of any kind, and if I had the means to buy cartridges, I'd have brought it to the quarry just to see if I could shoot me a mess of fish. But my visitor seemed restless, and to my great relief he soon left and climbed the steep path out of the quarry. It was years later, after I'd graduated high school, that I learned that the fellow was arrested by the FBI and confessed to plotting to blow up a bank in El Paso, Texas. On this occasion and one or two others, I could easily enough have ended up as a missing person with my face on a milk carton. As they say back in Letcher County, I wuz real damn lucky.

• • • • • • • •

Our house carried a mortgage of eight thousand dollars, and Mother can't have had any significant equity in it early on. It was pretty much what one would expect of an $8,000 house in the early 1950s. We had three bedrooms, a living room, and a kitchen, all sitting over a full basement, the basement being necessary if for no other reason than to accommodate the bulky coal-burning furnace with its eight heat ducts, each of which was a foot or more in diameter, and, incidentally, had asbestos wraps around the joints. Asbestos is now known to cause a lung disease called *mesothelioma*, but our pipe wraps were tight and solid, and I doubt that they sloughed off any bits that we might have breathed in.

Our house had previously sat on another site and it had been clad in weatherboard, but more recently it had been moved to its present site and covered with red imitation-brick siding. Two tall brick chimneys suggested the dormant fireplaces that had once heated the old house. The high walls of solid plaster on wood lathing showed many patches and not a few hairline cracks.

In any one room was enough heavy wood trim that if it were cut into what today is called "Ranch" trim, it would finish out an entire tract house in most new developments. Each solid wood panel door had a porcelain knob that was affixed to an escutcheon which had a keyhole that took a skeleton key. The light switches on the walls were the push-button type whose resistance to a finger push told you that inside were some hefty components. None ever failed, so we didn't have to find out if hardware stores still carried the things.

Our furnace dominated the basement space. A Hobart model sold by Sears and Roebuck, it was big and clunky, but except for not having an automatic stoker that would have avoided the need to attend it every couple of hours, it was up to date. Inside it two heavy iron grates moved in opposites directions to crush the "clinkers"—rock-like mineral residue of burning coal—when I heaved the long handle back and forth. I'd grab the cast iron handle that was almost as tall as me and had a knob the size of a baseball, and with both hands I'd heave it back and forth until all the ashes lay in the bottom where I could shovel them into a sixteen-gallon galvanized wash tub. I went one step at a time to lug the heavy tub up our open wooden steps and out the back door to the lot next door where nobody would mind our dumping, as it was already building up like a landfill from all the broken and discarded concrete burial vaults.

At the beginning of the heating season Marlowe Coal Company would deliver a load of large-lump coal. We'd remove a window from the foundation so the driver could sling the coal through it and let it clatter down into our basement coal bin.

I preferred the larger lumps because they seemed to burn longer than the same quantity in small lumps and I could make fewer trips down to throw on more coal. There were a few times when I came way too close to burning the house down. To save a trip to the basement, I'd overload the furnace, which in turn would cause the flue tube to glow cherry red and threaten to ignite the pine flooring just inches above where the red-hot tube connected with the cement–block portion of the chimney.

Our water heater was even then a relic, but it was a reliable relic and always did its job. Just as with the furnace, though, it was anything but automatic and had to be attended or else there'd be hell to pay. It was a "side-arm" design wherein the heater was apart from the tank. The heater, a copper coil heated by a gas burner, was enclosed inside a cylinder that had a hinged door for access; pipes connected it to the top and bottom of a copper tank that had a riveted seam up its side and was covered with the milky-green stain of copper oxidation. Convection caused the hot water to enter the top of the tank and the cold water in the bottom to flow to the heater coil and continue the cycle. I would feel the tank with a bare hand, and when it seemed warm enough, I'd turn off the gas and someone upstairs could take a bath, wash dishes, or whatever.

Sometimes we'd bathe or wash the dishes and forget to go back down to the basement and lower the flame in the heater, and that usually resulted in some excitement. The alert always came as one of us turned on a tap and was greeted by scalding steam that hissed and spat and told us to turn the heater off before the tank blew up. But the rivets always held and no one ended up scalded and disfigured like some unfortunate Irish immigrant child in an overcrowded tenement flat in New York's Hell's Kitchen.

We rode the city buses a lot before Manfred bought his first automobile, and I can say I enjoyed the experience. Even if I intended to go downtown, I'd catch the bus on its way out to the end of the line out at Cardinal Hill Hospital, the children's convalescent facility provided by the Shriners organization. The handsome facility still sits back from the road on a beautifully landscaped knoll at the corner of Versailles Road and Mason-Headly Road. I enjoyed the slow ride in the bus that allowed me time to study the pleasant surroundings, and I didn't mind sitting a few minutes when the driver had to kill time to get back on schedule, and I for sure didn't mind it when he had to tear out and make up for lost time. In the balmy springtime I would raise a window and prop an elbow on the ledge and feel the soft wind in my face.

Lexington's public transportation was one of the blessings of my childhood. The buses were great places for people-watching. Riders visited and chatted freely, and I listened in on adult conversations, about the weather of course, but also about local dignitaries and public figures, and not infrequently about one irascible driver in particular. I won't forget the time that an elderly black lady said of him for all to hear, "There's no fool like an old fool, and _____ is an old fool." "Old Fool" pretended not to hear, but he clamped his molars a little more firmly on the short stogie he kept parked in his right jaw and tromped hard on the accelerator to pin us back in our seats for a second and let us know who was captain of *that* ship.

Manfred bought his first car shortly before we left our apartment on East Fourth Street and moved out into the county to our new home on Halls Lane. It was a deep-green early 1940s Chevy coupe. With room for two in comfort, and four in a squeeze, it was pretty much just his "courting" car, but in the event of a medical emergency at least we could choose between the "Green Rocket" and a city bus.

Argie had a girlfriend, name of Hazel, and I liked Hazel. When a healthy eleven-year-old boy gets a little polite attention from an attractive young woman of twenty-one, what do you imagine takes place in his soft little developing brain? It wasn't that I "developed" a crush—anyone thinking that doesn't know how the brain functions in the head of an eleven-year-old boy. Nope, my brain didn't take time to "develop" anything; it sprang primed and loaded into secret sensual imaginings about that sweet little brunette. An author in need of material for a sleazy best-seller could do worse than plumb the frenzied imaginings of a pubescent lad in my state, caught as I was between Biblical proscriptions and the murky facts of life.

The pictorial content of men's magazines of the time was, I think, far more stimulating to the imagination than what passes for sexy photos in today's publications. The covers were all about male strength and virility, and many of them were variations on one theme. A muscular young fellow is wrapped in the sinewy coils of an overgrown Boa Constrictor, while in the background a nearly-naked goddess, bound hand and foot by jungle vines, slumps from a stout post, gasping and cringing in the certain knowledge that when the drums stop their pounding the natives will cease their mad dancing and sacrifice her to heathen gods.

The imaginative fiction inside stuck to recurring themes. The protagonists had names like Murphy and a habit of getting left behind on uncharted Pacific isles when the rest of Macarthur's troops pulled out after the Japanese surrender in Tokyo Bay. "Murphy" always had blonde hair, and that was all the natives required as proof that Murphy was their long-awaited god, a being who could do no wrong and who could be denied nothing, including his pick of the native women. As to how their stories ever made it out of those uncharted little kingdoms, I think that still remains a mystery.

Speaking of magazines, in Bill's Café was a news stand with all sorts of men's magazines, and on one unforgettable morning my young friends and I snuck a lingering look at *Playboy* as we hung out and waited for our school bus. To our delight and amazement, it was the famous issue featuring a reclining, carefully posed, nude Marilyn Monroe in the center-fold. I don't remember what we said about it, or if the sounds we made were even intelligible speech, but I believe we were unanimous in judging Miss Monroe superior to any naked pygmies we'd seen in the pages of *National Geographic* in the school library.

I spent a lot of my youth in Bill's Café. Bill's was housed in a modest-sized frame cottage that was a converted residence, and an asphalt-paved parking lot replaced what had once been a small front yard. Bill was big and genial, with a pudgy open face full of trust and acceptance. A hard worker, Bill didn't talk or lecture about what needed doing, he just tied his apron around his big soft middle and grabbed a spatula and showed how it was done. As a young man he quit his job as a grocery clerk in the store across the street and opened his first restaurant in a tiny frame building very near to the site he would move to next. There he gained a loyal following with his chili, bean soup, hamburgers, and affordable T-bone steaks, not to mention his rib-sticking breakfast platters. An astute businessman and affable host, Bill didn't remain long in the little hut before acquiring the cottage on the corner. With the added space, he was able to hire a staff of local women, all of whom brought with them not only cooking and serving skills but a host of friends and neighbors.

Bill never overlooked a way that he might use any available space to increase his revenue. He allowed Lexington's dominant novelty and entertainment company to install a juke box and two pinball machines. What boy with a dollar to spend wouldn't want a bowl of chili and a tall bottle of Pepsi, knowing he'd have some change left to play the pinball machine? The eastern wall wasn't doing anything but holding up that end of the roof, so he allowed Central Kentucky News, the local distributor of periodicals, to install a magazine rack in that space.

He never sought a license to sell alcohol of any kind; he didn't need it, he had all the business he could handle. In the early morning he fed a large breakfast crowd of folks on their way to work; horsemen and exercise riders from the nearby thoroughbred farms and Keeneland Race Track, deliverymen, and many of the hourly workers who'd catch the bus to their downtown jobs after they'd enjoyed the solid breakfasts that Bill kept moving from griddle to platter about as fast as the wait staff could set them in front of the hungry diners.

In my early days of frequenting Bill's Café I had no notion that I'd end up working for Bill and that the experience would figure so prominently in my adolescent development.

After two summers of mowing grass and doing odd jobs, my first regular job that paid hourly wages was in a restaurant. That was in the

Main street restaurant mentioned earlier, the one where my mother cooked during the evening shift. For two years I put in weekends there during the school year and then longer hours in the summer. At age thirteen, the first thing I had to do was to get a work permit for a minor. My mother and I took the bus to the offices of Lafayette Junior High School and got the paperwork handled.

That evening or the next, I reported to work. Mainly, I bussed tables and washed dishes. _____'s Restaurant had a prime Main Street location just a few doors west of Limestone Street, so they did a steady business. I stayed busy and the time actually passed pretty quickly for me. We didn't have an automatic dishwasher with a sterilizer—health department regulations were lax in that regard. What we had was a galvanized steel sink with three sections. In the first was hot soapy water, in the middle was the pre-rinse, and in the last was the scalding final rinse.

In my white apron that came down to my shoe tops, I'd go out to the tables with a deep metal tray and load it up with dirty dishes, glasses, and flatware. I'd wipe the table down and head back to the narrow kitchen, sliding past whoever was tending the griddle and on back to my steamy little corner.

There I'd remove each plate and use a tire brush to swipe the plate and send the food remnants through a hole in the galvanized counter top and down into the "slop" can. At closing time I hauled the slop can to the curb for pickup by an African-American pig farmer who hoisted it into the trunk of his '52 Ford sedan and, with his rear bumper just clearing the pavement, made off down West Main, to where, I was never to learn. My final duty of the night was to sweep and mop the Terrazzo tile floor. Even then I knew to use scalding hot water and plenty of soap so as not to leave the floor slippery, as they are today in so many fast food joints tended by youth who've never been required, or even permitted, to learn any domestic skills at home.

I was conscientious about getting my dishes sparkling clean—and I did it for fifty cents an hour—but I suspected that overall sanitation could have been improved. There was too much stuff in too close proximity to other stuff. Still, we served some very palatable dishes, and none of our customers complained of gastric distress that might be laid to our practices, even though I believed one of our practices to be that of the boss bribing the health inspector; not paying him to overlook blatant health hazards, no, but to go easy on the picky stuff. Hell, we knew that just because a can of scouring powder sat on a ledge above the potato-peeling station nobody would be fool enough to mistake it for salt. And the same went for quart jugs of vinegar and Pine-Sol; no fool would ever confuse those two, would they?

Bits of unwanted stuff are bound to make their way into food that's processed in vast lots, and our federal government has decreed just how much of various types of matter is allowable. Three categories I know of are rat hair, rat shit, and insect parts. If you eat peanut butter, even if it's a gourmet brand, you can believe that you've consumed at least minute quantities of these things. And did you complain? I doubt that you did. And yet picture the customer's outrage and dismay the time in our restaurant when one of them found a used Band-Aid in his Cole Slaw. There was hell to pay, and why not? There it was— ugh, yuck, p-tooey. The positive view of the matter, which the customer was understandably blind to, was that a bandage is at least detectable, and you can send the disgusting dish back to the kitchen. Shit happens, in the best of dining establishments, but in the places I worked no one ever fainted or brought a lawsuit. I don't remember, but I do hope, however, that our unfortunate diner turned the place blue with loud swearing.

I had a huge crush on one chubby waitress who had curly, kind of frizzy, blond hair. Maybe it was because she didn't seem at all worldly and didn't have the glib tongue of our older waitresses; she was a country girl and it showed, but in a way that I learned later is irresistible to men. Her bearing suggested that a man could flirt without fear of an ego-deflating rebuff. But I wasn't a man, and I didn't make that assessment back then. She was sweet, and she didn't know how softly alluring she was, and she may have sensed that I mooned over her, I don't know, but, oh, how I wished to be a few years older.

I worked a couple of years at _____'s, and then my mother applied and was accepted as kitchen help at the new IBM plant out on New Circle Road on the north side of town. I remember the picture in the paper of Governor Happy Chandler turning the first spade of earth at what was to be IBM's new facility for manufacturing typewriters. When Mother left her old job at _____'s, I left with her, and by the next summer I was flipping burgers at Bill's Café. No bus ride to work, just the hundred yards or so from our house to Bill's, where I waited on people I knew. I started out on weekends, washing dishes and helping another part-timer to peel potatoes. Joe Hartman seemed old to me then, but he held down a regular job in maintenance at the

Bluegrass Ordinance Depot in Richmond, Kentucky. I liked working with jovial Joe and listening to his gentle teasing and joshing with the female help. Peeling potatoes and cutting them into crinkle fries was my actual food-handling job. That and using an ice cream scoop to shape ground beef into balls that the grill person would take a heavy spatula to and smash into flat burger patties.

Bill's was much more than just a place for me to earn fifty cents an hour doing a fun job; it was an important stop in my lifelong education in cookery and added to the kitchen influences of Mary Calihan, of my mother, of my Norwegian mother-in-law and of others along the way. I never stopped cooking, and with the help of recipes on the Worldwide Web, I'm still exploring, and, if I have to say so, I'm cooking better than ever. I spoil myself terribly and can only be lured to eat out if it's a social occasion.

.

1956-57: Me and a pretty coworker behind the counter at Bill's Café. I know the year because I'm wearing my sweetheart's class ring on a chain around my neck. The pay wasn't much, but short-order cooking was easy and the juke box played continuously, a little bit of Patti Page and a whole lot of Elvis and his Rockabilly contemporaries Jerry Lee Lewis, Carl Perkins, and Johnny Cash.

It was a short season for No. 62.

23 Three Good years

I stayed out of trouble for most of my time at Lafayette Junior High, and I made good grades, and I began to think that I wasn't so dumb after all. My seventh-grade teacher, Mrs. Katherine Wilkie, won my complete respect and lasting regard. She authored some juvenile fiction about notable figures on the American Frontier: Daniel Boone, Zachary Taylor, and others. I loved learning from "Miz" Wilkie, and I learned how good it felt to be encouraged and rewarded for my efforts. I was proud, and possibly a little smug, the time she sent me into the cloakroom to tutor another boy in reading. On another occasion I was first proud and happy but soon afterward embarrassed and crestfallen.

I was proud to win the home-room spelling bee, and I was delighted when Miz Wilkie gave me the keys to her car and sent me and a classmate out to bring back the prize I'd won. I was excited to find in the back seat of the car a wrapped box tied up in a pretty ribbon. I took no note of the humble little container that sat on the package ledge behind the back seat.

On returning to the classroom Miz Wilkie took one look and said with a sigh, "No, no, that's a present for my mother. Take it back and bring the small container." We made the switch and returned with a little box in which was about a dozen pieces of homemade fudge. It was thoughtful of our kind teacher, but this was not the mystery gift I'd gotten so excited about.

When the occasion called for it, Miz Wilkie would leave the prescribed curriculum to lecture us, especially the boys, on the rudiments of respectable behavior. In 1951, grape-flavored chewing gum, branded "Grape Gum", ranked high among the sugary treats favored by kids. Some knot-head of a boy thought how clever it might be to tear off the initial G and offer a female classmate a stick of "rape" gum, or to just leave one lying on the floor by her desk and then wait for her to notice, at which time the boys would exchange knowing smirks, provided Miz Wilkie had her back to the classroom.

Then one day as we were settling down upon returning from lunch break, Miz Wilkie dismissed the girls and had them wait in the hall. Just the boys remained in the room, just us guilty "perps" and Miz Wilkie, who folded her arms and stood still as a statue for a while and beheld us with a sad countenance. We were goners and we knew it. We just prayed it wasn't about "rape" gum. We'd just die if this sweet, tolerant lady knew the sordid story and felt she must descend to our level to deal with it.

How much easier it would have been for us if she'd launched into a tirade and berated us with a proper "woodshed" lecture. But that wasn't her style. Miz Wilkie conducted herself with all propriety, the most dignified lady I'd encountered so far in my young life.

We learned much more than just the plain fact that we had created a hostile learning environment. With her carefully chosen words, delivered with utter calm, she stretched our appreciation for the power of language. She didn't threaten or harangue, didn't say that we were awful, and didn't leave us feeling we'd committed some unpardonable sin. She allowed us some shred of hope that we were redeemable and ended with just enough of a smile for us to know, if we'd been discerning enough to realize it, that she had us right where she wanted us and wouldn't have any more problems from us for the rest of that term.

As I think of my eighth grade teacher, Mr. Donaldson, and what a good man and effective teacher he was, I feel such gratitude that I had superlative teachers at every grade, from the primer right on through high school. It's too late to lament my failure to make the most of that time. It's just that writing about that time brings it into clear focus and fills me with gratitude for the learning environment that was mine and that I so wish could be the same for today's children in public schools. Not that our curriculum couldn't have been improved upon or that instruction methods were up to today's standards, but, damn it—and I don't mean to preach—I looked forward to the school day, rarely felt threatened by any of my peers, and never experienced the sort of classroom bedlam that turns teachers into wardens and so undermines the goals of public education. It is something to remember and be grateful for.

In one of my several jobs since retiring I spent three years as a substitute teacher at Henderson County (Kentucky) High School. There I learned enormous respect for the dedicated teaching staff and for the administrators, all of whom it seems face a more difficult task than did my teachers back in the 1950s. Having said that, I do think, however, that my old teachers would have been up to the task of educating today's youth. Mr. Donaldson—who shared with his students the fact that he'd shortened his surname by leaving off the "Mc" prefix just to make his name handier, and not by any means to deny his proud Scottish heritage—would have been right at home in front of a group of eighth-graders in any of today's tough urban middle schools.

Mr. D was short and rotund with a round face that seemed always on the verge of sharing some revealing aside. He never bored us, and yet he kept his lectures on topic. There were times when he would have been justified in paddling me and a cohort for our schemes to infuriate a classmate who was funniest when he was angry. I could tell about it, and some would be amused to hear it, but our classmate, who grew to become a community leader, deserves better than to be reminded.

Seventh and eighth grades, that's all there was to Lafayette Junior High, but that's just two of what I remember as three good years. Ninth grade meant I was in high school, but the big high school building was just to the other side of that same campus I'd been coming to since the fifth grade, so I was familiar with my surroundings. I say it was another good year mostly because I was still associating with my pals that lived close to where I lived on Halls Lane and had been my friends since the fifth grade. I wasn't yet running around with anyone who had their own car, and I wasn't skipping school. I hadn't yet traded in the good feeling that comes with having done my homework for the feeling of belonging that came from joining a loose group that was experimenting with rebellion. I liked my teachers, and since I was still pretty uniformly compliant, they seemed to approve of me.

Without a doubt, the ninth grade was a good year. Homeroom first thing in the morning; roll call followed by devotions that included Bible reading and prayer followed by the Pledge of Allegiance, and then we dispersed to the various classrooms for actual learning. Our ninth grade homeroom teacher, Mr. Ferguson, was well liked by the boys and drooled over by the girls. Fresh out of college, where he was named "Little All American" for his quarterback play for the Murray State Thoroughbreds, Mr. Ferguson was the square-jawed picture of good health and clean living, a composite of all things that landed college jocks from larger football factories than his Alma Mater on the cover of sports magazines. Flat stomach, narrow necktie tucked in at his waist, quite handsome in his sandy-haired crew-cut, Mr. Ferguson had us eating out of his hand, and so I think it was easy for him to be the student's friend, always charming, never scolding.

My memory of him is so much in contrast to the other high school teachers, mostly women, whose chore it was to lecture and try to make us learn English, Math, and the sciences. Not all of them had fiercely black hair tied in a tight bun with a pencil run through it, nor did they all have a pair of glasses hanging from a lanyard and resting on an ample bosom. Perhaps that image is only because of how I for so long recalled Mrs. B, the drama teacher. Yes, she had black braids wrapped tight against her skull, but I never actually saw a pencil sticking in her hair, and she was, on reflection, fit and trim looking. But, she loomed so tall and menacing whenever she found me stretching the minutes in the hallway between classes as I delayed my girlfriend from reaching her next class on time. If I remember Mrs. B growling at me to "Git, you little heathen," as I know very well she did no such thing, it's only because I've repressed the memory of how I put on adult airs for my beloved and how deflated I was every time she had to witness a teacher putting me in my hated little juvenile place. Young love, that helpless devotion of a smitten young swain—call it terminal neediness—from my tortured experience, is a real bitch.

In addition to coaching her young thespians and whipping them into shape for Gilbert and Sullivan's *HMS Pinafore*, or Rodgers and Hammerstein's *Oklahoma*, and other productions about which I knew nothing and cared less at the time, Mrs. B directed the school's singing groups, *Charmettes* being the girls, and *Chanteurs* the boys. To me, Mrs. B's students represented a fortunate segment of the student body that was distinguished by their good clothes, pretty white teeth, and other marks attesting to homes where children were well provided for. I had no desire to enter that rarified realm, or, perhaps I repressed a strong desire to belong and pretended sour grapes all the way because it would have hurt to want what could not be mine. So I privately sneered at anyone with so little manly pride as to wear makeup and croon a love song to a pretty classmate made up to be a Victorian beauty. Still, as the auditorium lights dimmed and the players took the spotlight, I lost myself in the performance, grudgingly admiring the classmate cast as the lead character and sensing vaguely that here was an opportunity to glimpse a finer part of life than what I'd so far allowed myself to see.

From Tenth grade on, Mrs. L was my homeroom teacher, and except for an occasional transfer in or out, our tenth grade group remained intact for those three years. Based on what was barely evident then but more pronounced in the adults we turned out to be, I'd say we were as good a cross-section of Lafayette Senior High School as could have been assembled by a team of experts. We had our rebel, our very own "Fonzy", with slicked-back dark hair and always a white T-shirt with the sleeves rolled into a tight tube that delineated his prominent collar bone from his lean shoulders and stringy biceps. When he was away from the classroom, one sleeve of his Tee bulged with the outline of a cigarette pack. James S. was "cool" before the word itself was cool, a mouthy transfer from either Philly or New Jersey, exotic, and secretly admired for his fresh-mouthed repartee that skated so close to taunting anyone in authority. We had our buffoon, our achievers, our dormice—if that word be the plural of dormouse—our actors-out, and our clinically-detached observers. I see myself as having been in the middle ground, flexible while leaning somewhat toward miscreant behavior, and seeking approval without being terribly concerned about from whence it came.

I was also in love, and laying the foundation for decades of fluctuating inner turmoil that I came to pursue like a hobby was the fact that I was devoid of accurate, serviceable, meaningful self-knowledge. I had not a scintilla of true inner awareness, only false or misleading notions about myself. Callow and needy I was, and the fact that I survived has to be owing entirely to the girl with whom I was so desperately in love, the pretty, trusting girl with a 100-watt smile, the girl I married when we were just one year out of high school. I credit her with making the good part of the man that was thereafter to inhabit my body.

I had gone out for football in the eighth grade and did well enough to make the Jayvee team. At 150 pounds I played in the line and both gave and received the pounding that went with this unglamorous role. I believe I was fast enough to have been a ball carrier, but I was reticent in the face of the boys who saw the backfield as their natural domain, so I was happy enough just to be knocking heads in the trenches.

In the ninth grade I was still on the Jayvee team, but I was permitted to dress out for the varsity's post-season "bowl" game, which, prior to the formation of classes of sports teams based on enrollment numbers, was a match between the two top-ranked teams in the state. My uniform included a beat up practice helmet and pants so baggy they had to be taped around my legs to prevent them ballooning out like a clown suit, but, what the heck, I wasn't going to be let onto the field in such an important game, and no one paid any attention to a bunch of grunts at the end of the bench.

We'd won the big game by a close score and were on the bus headed back to our motel rooms when I had an experience that might have foretold where my behavior was headed. Had I the experience and insight to properly analyze it, I'd have seen that something about my bearing invited others to include me in their delinquency. I sat in the far back of the bus, and it happened that our star player, for reasons soon revealed, had also opted to sit back there away from the coaches in the front of the bus.

Donald P. was two grades ahead of me and, athletically speaking, on another planet altogether, so I didn't think twice when he pulled a half pint bottle of whiskey from the pocket of his long gabardine topcoat and knocked the poison off of it before passing it to me.

By the time school resumed on Monday morning, I had mentally demoted myself from the varsity team, which after all had been for one day only, and I had no thought of participating in the convocation that was planned to celebrate the victory that saw Lafayette High School declared the "mythical" state football champion. The regular varsity players stood at the end of the gym, but I was in the stands with kids from my homeroom when legendary coach Paul "Bear" Bryant, then the coach for the University of Kentucky, took center stage to congratulate the Lafayette Generals. When Bryant concluded his remarks, our coach started down the roster in alphabetical order calling the name of each player, whereupon the named player would step forward to the applause of his fellow students. As our coach neared my letter of the alphabet, I secretly hoped he'd go on past and not mention my name; I wasn't even a footnote to our great victory. But call my name he did, and I who had not made it onto the playing field had to make a "grand entrance". I'm sure I was blushing furiously as I edged my way along the bleachers and down the steps and then across the hardwood to take my place with the team. I was in bad need of a haircut, and my attire was just an average selection from my below-average wardrobe. I had wanted to belong, but right then I would have preferred to be invisible. I had no desire to put myself above what I perceived as my place in the order of things.

I was attached to various groups, none of which was a gang as gangs are today constituted. There were no requirements for membership, with the possible exception of seeing oneself as an outsider. My pals and I were outsiders in the larger scene, and so I think we had to make our status one that we could take some solace in. We drank a little at times, and occasionally we perpetrated some minor thefts, but mostly we stuck together as a means of providing for each other the approbation that wasn't coming from our participation in groups and events that were beyond our social reach.

In the ninth grade I'd taken a morning paper route that required me to leave my warm bed about three hours earlier than normal. Naturally, I arrived sleep-deprived and groggy for my first-period Algebra class, and just as naturally, I came very close to flunking the class. The worst of it was that I decided I was no good at math, and in the tenth grade this proved a self-fulfilling prophecy. I should have cracked a book every night and sought help at school, but no, I chose to skip school on a fairly regular basis and pay the price of shame and humiliation when called upon to write a Geometry exercise on the blackboard. Time lost its wings, each second held its place and let go grudgingly, as I near suffocated under the pitying gaze of twenty-five pairs of eyes.

Such painful experience was best forgotten, or so I thought, but like a fiend with his dope, I had to have my regular time with my misguided friends. I craved their approval that came so reliably; it must have been worth it to me at the time to betray my native intelligence and buy time with my bosom pals.

We were not the disadvantaged youth of today's inner-city warrens of crime and despair, and I'm sure I can't truly imagine all the dangers and hardships in those places, but I believe I do understand some of why many young people join gangs.

A football team is hardly a gang, but being a member of one filled the same sort of need for me as did my running with the juvenile delinquents in my neighborhood. Football meshed together boys from the model households with those from the single-parent, barely-getting-by households. Our coaches were like military drill sergeants in that they didn't give a damn about whose papa was a bum or whose was a doctor; they cared only about who could block, or tackle, or hold on to the football, and who could thrive on pain. And, by and large, the boys themselves held the same view, at least for those periods when markers of social strata were blurred by our uniforms. Being a football player gave me some visibility in the hallways of Lafayette High, and there were times when I didn't feel I was so different from others, times when I wasn't overly conscious of my shabby wardrobe. If I could have dressed better, if my outward appearance had been more like that of my classmates, then I think that I might have harvested more warm memories from my high school experience. But if you mend holes in your socks with white adhesive tape and use a pen and ink to darken the patch and you just know that not only is the patch noticeable but your efforts to hide it are even more so, well, that kind of shitty little detail will take the swagger out of most fifteen-year-old boys.

I learned easily enough, but mathematics and the laboratory sciences never interested me as much as did the written word and liberal studies. I was an avid reader even at the time I was skipping school, and I garnered teacher praise for papers I would write. By my junior year I was pleased to be writing English theme papers for my sweetheart. She wouldn't think of skipping school, and she'd have gasped and fainted dead away under a scrunched-brow, beady-eyed scolding from a teacher, but all that goodness didn't make my beloved a scholar.

I could give her almost nothing that cost money, but I could give what I had, and what I had to give was what sprang from my embryonic love of language. We shared an English class that was taught by one of the most popular teachers in the school, and I was far from chagrined the day that Mr. H asked me if I was writing papers for my sweetheart. He never directly accused, this wise and understanding man, as he had no unassailable proof. He just let me know that he was no fool. And I rejoiced at the indirect praise that came from one whom I admired for his literary worldliness. The grudging "C" that turned up on papers submitted by my sweetheart was received with our joint gratitude. C wasn't as good as the B, or the occasional A, that the papers would have merited had they actually been her work, but our teacher knew what was what, and my dear one was well enough pleased to get those Cs.

In April of 1955 I turned sixteen with no thought of getting a driver's license. My oldest brother had a car, a brand new 1955 Plymouth Savoy, green and white two-tone, automatic transmission with the shift lever sticking out of the dashboard. It was a dashing ride for a young man, a fine courting car, but there was no point in him teaching me to drive since I would not have a car of my own until I could buy one from my own earnings. My part-time restaurant job paid me fifty cents an hour, and I spent it all on food and bus fare.

I rode the city buses across town to see my beloved, where we'd sit at her mom's kitchen table and drink cokes and split a bag of potato chips. I went courting by bus so regularly that I got to know the bus drivers, and they got to know my routine and were supportive, to the point of kindly Mr. Stivers stopping several houses before the designated stop and letting me off in front of her house. At other times, a good friend that lived on my block and had a car of his own was kind enough to invite me and my sweetie to double date.

One benefit of double dating was that we could stay out past 11:00 PM and know that I wouldn't be walking home after missing the last bus of the night. This happened to me from time to time when I'd take the bus across town to see my dear one. Sometimes I just couldn't tear myself away in time to catch the last bus, and I'd face a four-mile walk home. Four miles was as nothing; I'd gladly have walked twice the distance, but distance wasn't the problem. The problem was that I had to pass through some dark neighborhoods, loading docks and the backs of poorly lighted commercial buildings, and then cross over two viaducts, one of which took me past Irishtown, a poverty-ridden section of town where if I had seen anyone about late at night I'd have run in the opposite direction and found some place where I could wait for daylight to come.

• • • • • • • •

1955 was an eventful year for me. I lied about my age and joined the National Guard. Some of my older football buddies joined the Guard, and that's where I wanted to be, doing manly things, hanging with guys that to some degree shared my proclivity for testing the bounds of acceptable youth behavior. On Wednesday nights at the Armory, I enjoyed the rigor and the newfound sense of purpose and was more readily compliant with authority than was true of any other of my group memberships besides football. I wanted some stripes on the sleeves of my fatigue uniform shirt and saw that compliance was the best way to go about getting them

I remember 1955 also for one iconic moment on a fall afternoon. The football team was to play a rare Saturday afternoon game, and I'd ridden the city bus from home to the Lafayette campus. As I stepped off the bus with my just-polished black cleats strung around my neck, I beheld an automobile of such stunning new design that I could only stand in wonder and amazement. It was a 1955 Chevrolet Bel Air Two-Tone Hardtop Coupe, maroon and white. GM had worked a wonder and broken forever from the utilitarian look of what they'd heretofore been putting in America's driveways.

As for football, my junior year found me in a kind of limbo. Juniors didn't play jayvee, and the varsity was loaded with senior talent, so I mostly just sat on the bench. But that was just during our actual scheduled games; I had a grand old time at practices, especially during the pre-season. In August the team boarded school buses and rode to Sparta, Tennessee to a Boy Scout Ranch. There we bunked four to a cabin, ate our meals in a mess hall, and had a lake and canoes at our disposal. That was the recreational side of things. The business at hand was practice twice a day under a broiling hot sun.

When a player got very red in the face and bent over to vomit his breakfast, we thought, oh well, he has a stomach bug, he'll get over it. Neither we nor our coaches knew squat about heat stroke, and our coaches, ignorant in the matter of proper hydration, denied us drinking water during the practices. They didn't want us to "bloat". Luckily, no one died or even required hospitalization. Well, they most likely did *require* hospitalization, but that wasn't going to happen with a group of coaches who shared the same "death march" approach to conditioning that Coach Bear Bryant espoused.

Our big men suffered, but I wasn't fazed. I had arrived weighing 160 pounds and would leave weighing 150 pounds. I was fit, I wasn't carrying any blubber. My happy experience here left me with a sense of belonging that stood up during a season of riding the bench, a season that saw our talented seniors, including my brother Jim playing end, win almost all their games and hold on to Lafayette's reputation as a football power.

Away from school and the playing field I spent my weekends behind the counter at Bill's Café, where I was pretty competent as a short-order cook and waiter. Bill's eatery served our neighborhood and beyond, offering warmth and easy hospitality and doing a bustling trade. It should have been a good place for me to mature and get some direction in my life, and maybe it was, but there were temptations.

One Saturday, Mrs. R., who made the chili and the bean soup, called me aside to say that one of her customers who drove a truck for a liquor distributor had left her a half-pint of whiskey as a tip and that she really didn't like that brand of whiskey, so she'd leave it for me. I came on duty in the early afternoon along with Mrs. W., a chirpy and grandmotherly little neighbor lady. Traffic was slow until the early evening, and I decided to sample the hidden booze.

Shortly afterward a young couple came in and I took their order and put some burgers on the griddle and dropped a basket of fries in the cooker. And that's all I remember until I heard Mrs. W. holler, "Whose hamburgers are these burning on the grill?" Damned if I knew. There was just the two of us on duty, and the burgers weren't mine, so they had to be hers. What was wrong with that woman? Then the fog cleared a bit. Aargh! Oh shit, those are my damn burgers.

Mrs. W., bless her, let me stew in my own juices—I served the burgers and straightened myself up some—but, God love her, she didn't rat me out to the boss, nor, so far as I know, did she tell my mother, who was Mrs. W.'s friend and sometime confidant. I reckon that abetting a semi-delinquent is an easy path to social bonding, but I in no way wish to demean any adult that took this path to connect with me. To the extent that some adult acquaintances did so, I think they are to be forgiven. If they were going to influence me for the good, then they had first to win my trust, and they were just proceeding from the little they knew about such matters. After all, they didn't have Dr. Phil to correct their misguided notions about adult influence on troubled youths. So I reject any high-minded flak about bad adult influences. It would have been a different matter if they'd been undermining the parenting efforts of Ward and June Cleaver. My beleaguered mother had little time and even less energy to devote to correcting my unpromising behavior, so it was largely up to me to stir the influences, good and bad, and choose among them.

Scholastically speaking, my senior year was about the same as the year before. I excelled in a few courses and stunk in one or two. Mrs. L was both my homeroom teacher and my Geometry teacher, and I think she liked me. That's the only way I can explain the D she gave me in the final grading period, when I'd done everything needed to earn an F. That D let me escape with a D for the semester. Mrs. L must have known that I needed to work and earn some money over the summer and that I couldn't afford to be attending summer school. Besides, she had every right to assume that this boy wasn't headed for any college that would admit him, so what did it matter?

Athletically, my senior year was an unmitigated disaster, for me and for the football team. We'd graduated a ton of beef in the line and everyone else who was any good at the skill positions, quarterback, running back, and pass catchers. We were small all across the front line, on offense and defense, except for our center, who was a big strong fellow, and also one of the most upstanding lads in our group. I think it was in the second game of the season when Big Bill dislocated a shoulder and was out for the season. Who was left that could snap the ball? Anyone could line up at center and slap the ball into the quarterback's hands when those widespread hands were firmly up against the center's family jewels. But who could make the long snap to the punter? That was a critical issue because we were "three and out" in most of our offensive series, which is to say, we often failed to move the ball forward ten yards in three attempts to make a first down and were left with the choice of making a fourth attempt, and possibly failing to make a first down, or just punting the ball to set our opponents a little further back from their goal.

Our coach, a good man but a slave driver in the mold of his old coach, Bear Bryant, gave us all a shot at making the long snap. When it came my turn, I knew that form mattered and that confidence was called for. I leaned out and put some weight on the ball, gripping it so as to put a spiral on it, and then I heaved it between my legs for the ten yards or so back to the waiting punter. It looked like I'd been doing it for a while, and that's all it took, I had the job. I was small at 150 pounds, but I was what ESPN pundits call "coachable".

For the next two games I had some hits and misses. Making the short snaps was easy enough, and because I was light and agile I generally carried through with my blocking assignment. But in a tough game against Louisville Manual we were in a hole offensively and needed to punt out of trouble. The pressure got to me, and I forgot all I knew about making the long snap. I bounced the ball back in the general direction of our punter, and a Manual player scooped it up and ran it in for a touchdown. I was put out with myself, and our coach was pulling his hair and stomping along the sidelines, but who could he put in? No one else had shown any promise in practice.

Coach liked me for the effort I gave. I played at linebacker on defense, and because our defensive front was so porous, I made a lot of pursuit tackles, which if they accomplished nothing else, they kept our opponents' scores down to something we could take some hope from.

My personal calamity came in our fifth game of the season. The Somerset Briar Jumpers—yep that's their name, or it was back then, and they were proud of it—were our opponents. Late in the first half of a fairly even contest the Jumpers blocked with devastating effect and opened a big hole in our line, right in front of me. The ball carrier didn't zig, and he didn't zag, he just barreled straight toward me. I held my ground and didn't rush forward lest he give me a fake and slip past me. When we met, the momentum was all his and he fell forward in my grasp. I stopped the play but paid a price. I landed hard on my back, with the calves of my legs lined up precisely beneath my thighs. It wouldn't have mattered what was aligned with what, except that three of my teammates had escaped their blockers and piled on top of me and the ball carrier. There I was on the bottom of the pile with several hundred pounds of meat bearing down on my thighs. Beneath my right thigh my right foot had nowhere to go. With the toe of my low-cut cleats wedged firmly in the soggy turf and my heel mashed nearly up into my thigh bone, something had to give. And it did. Toe cleats touched heel cleats, and three metatarsals, the ones between my big and little toes, cracked and splintered like green twigs.

As we unpiled I felt no immediate pain, just a sickening limpness in my right foot and a feeling that my shoe was laced exceedingly tight. That was the instantaneous swelling. We had a stretcher on the sideline, but that was just for appearance sake, probably just in compliance with the rules of the state high school athletic association. No Lafayette General would be toted off the field like a WWI Doughboy being taken from No Man's Land. Instead I limped off with the support of two teammates, my rubbery-feeling foot just dangling, a foreign-feeling appendage.

Our team doctor hauled me to the emergency room in his Cadillac, and he didn't have the decency to tune his radio to the play-by-play. Which was just as well, as I learned next day that we'd lost the game.

On Saturday afternoon, October 8, 1956, I was drugged up and sitting in the TV room of a ward at Lexington's Central Baptist Hospital. A cast covered my right leg up to the knee, and it rested on the fold-out support of my wheel-chair. In the open end of the cast, between my toes, the turned-up ends of three coarse wires indicated the repairs that had been done. My shattered metatarsals were aligned on skewers.

On top of that depressing situation, I was too groggy from pain killers to fully appreciate that an historic baseball game was being shown on the TV. Pitcher Don Larsen of the New York Yankees was pitching what was then and has remained the only perfect game in World Series history, and he was doing it against my boyhood favorites, the Brooklyn Dodgers. As I said, it was just a pure calamity in every possible way.

For the next six weeks I stumbled through the halls of Lafayette on crutches. The bright side was that I got out early from my final period class and my girlfriend and wife-to-be also got out early so she could come by my classroom and carry my books out to my bus.

While on crutches I ate the same as ever and I wasn't getting any exercise, so my weight shot up from about 160 pounds to 185 pounds. And whereas I had previously stuck to the training rules during the football season, I now began smoking in earnest. I went to the next two games to encourage my teammates, but the whole thing was just too depressing, and I failed to attend the last couple of games. My injured foot was tender and the crutches were a bother, but it was selfish of me to blow off those two games.

Graduation night was a vain search for excitement, and a protracted one at that. With no car of my own, I had to content myself with going wherever my ride took me. I did manage to get drunk, and that in some small measure scratched my rebellious itch and helped me pretend that I wouldn't have gone to any damn old party even if I'd been invited. Actually, though, I wasn't lonely, for the lower teenage caste that I belonged to was sizable, especially out in the west end of Lexington, and I was among friends as we feinted at challenging the *status quo*, drinking, joking, and bitching as the night wore down.

After graduation, Jim and I spent the summer working for a painting contractor. Our boss was a likable fellow, and we didn't know to object when he put us up on church cupolas and up among steel I-beams high above gymnasium floors, all without benefit of safety harnesses of any kind. It would have been a blatant violation of OSHA rules had OSHA been around at the time. I liked the boss's brother. He could drive his stick shift truck and roll and light a homemade cigarette as he worked the shifter and gesticulated wildly with one or both hands. And he knew some disgusting dirty jokes, the fine fellow.

I am struck by the general appearance and conduct of house painters today—they seem positively normal. Our crew included winos and the occasional travelling man, a working hobo, of sorts, that the boss would pick up from the informal day-labor pool on one particular downtown street corner. The crew all liked me well enough to devote their considerable talents to educating me in all behaviors crude and deplorable.

But one of our crew was a hymn-singing Nazarene who I came to admire for his unflappability as he let slide off his back all the scurrilous bleating of one young knucklehead and his filthy-tongued older brother. They taunted poor Herbert about whores, bestiality, and any other depravity their fertile imaginations could conjure up.

That my young friends in our neighborhood weren't just as dirty-minded as my painter friends was attributable to the former's abysmal ignorance of female anatomy. Here, the painters filled the gap admirably and fired my desire to learn a great deal more on the topic.

I'd been raised by a widowed mother, and the company of men that I'd heretofore enjoyed was for the most part that of my uncles. I deemed them useless as a source of knowledge of the kind that a young boy would not get from his mother. But there was one notable exception, and that was my beloved Uncle Isaac, from whom I learned so much by observing how a good man conducted himself. I also learned from him that a good man could have a sense of humor and communicate that part of himself to a growing boy.

.

Top Left: My University of Kentucky Senior photo, 1962. Top Right: ready for UK v. Penn State in the 1999 Outback Bowl in Tampa, FL. Bottom: Fishing in south-central Kentucky, 2012.

24 Fast Forward

At the end of my eighteenth summer, if I didn't have the mental or physical powers of a man I nevertheless faced some man-sized choices, and no adult that I knew was going make the choices for me, nor were they able to offer more than minimal material support for the adult undertakings that I was ill-equipped to take on.

But, take them on I did. And from that point until much more recently is a time that I may never write about. For one thing, my children, now into their own mid-lives, know it as well as, if not better than, I do. And for another thing, I feel so changed now from the man I was throughout all that time that to revisit it seems pointless. So I will close with just a few words about the past ten years.

Ten years ago my son, the youngest of my children, died leaving an infant son and a grieving young mother. In the immediate sad aftermath of our great loss I remained at the place I'd retired to, but within a year's time I left my retirement plans behind and came to be near them, for what turned out to be our mutual support. In just a matter of a few weeks, as I engaged with my infant grandson and his heart-broken mother, I came slowly to regard myself in a different light.

Perhaps I'd simply worn out all my old ways and was unknowingly looking entirely outside of myself to find a new way forward. I may not be the one to judge whether or not I have truly changed, but that's how it feels from the inside.

I have questioned whether the change is real, or if it is just a sense of peace that comes and goes and cannot be trusted to last. With that thought in mind, I will tell now of something unexpected and deeply gratifying that happened recently.

My youngest grandson shows every sign of becoming the same sort of capable and caring man his father was. Open-minded and articulate beyond his twelve years, his interests span a good deal more than just texting his young friends and being on the go. We were in my car, on our way to one of his youth football practices, just Jackson and his grandpa, or "Pappy", as I've been called ever since my first grandchild thus named me. My grandson asked of me, "Pappy, how come I've never seen you angry?"

As I considered the implication of his question, I had to ask myself if his understanding fit the facts. With only seconds to ponder it, I did a quick mental search, and as I was unable to recall ever actually losing my composure in front of him, I gratefully accepted that if anyone would have taken note of anger on my part it would have been my sensitive and observant grandson. I accepted his take on the matter for the gift it was and knew I'd treasure the moment as long as I live.

The end

Afterword

My story has been mainly about my childhood, with an occasional mention of later developments, and it ends with my reaching adulthood, but some may wish to know how others of my family have fared since that time. I'm only too glad to share a happy ending with them.

Everyone in my family was tested, but we can each one look back and say we were fortunate. We emerged from the worst of it healthy and whole and with not much standing between us and the opportunities that awaited us, and then we went on to enjoy better times that have lasted many years. We ended up in good places: with good educations, successful careers, and children we can be proud of. Our mother got to see all her grand-children grow into adulthood and got to see one great-grandchild. She enjoyed ten years of retirement in Florida, living with her oldest surviving daughter, until she left us for good in 1985. Since then we've held family gatherings every other year, first in the Ozark Mountains, then on the Gulf Coast of Florida, and more recently on the shores of Lake Barkley in western Kentucky. We are four generations now, and while we are all linked by blood or by marriage to the woman who left the hills of eastern Kentucky to find her future, what binds us now is the simple joy we take in knowing and caring for each other.

ABOUT THE AUTHOR

Forester Hogg was born on Kings Creek, in Letcher County, Kentucky, and moved soon after to the nearby village of Roxana. It was here, and in places close by, that he lived for his first ten years. He graduated from the University of Kentucky with a BA in Sociology. After completing a career-long detour through the field of computer software development, he has turned his attention back to what originally lay behind his interest in Sociology—the culture of his Appalachian birthplace. In his lifetime he has seen rural Appalachia lose much of its centuries-old identity under the culture-leveling influence of increased educational opportunity, popular media, access to the Internet, and easy travel. His purpose in writing *Roxana* has been to depart from the aims of scholars and TV documentaries and tell a personal story of the richly-textured life he experienced in the hills of eastern Kentucky.

Made in the USA
Charleston, SC
06 October 2013